HISTORY'S SHOCKING SECRETS

A *"Twist In Time"* Book

HISTORY'S SHOCKING SECRETS
A *"Twist In Time"* Book

BILL COATE

HISTORY PUBLISHING GROUP
FRESNO, CALIFORNIA

For more information address History Publishing Group, Inc.,
5588 N. Palm Avenue #112, Fresno, CA 93705
P. O. Box 27288 Fresno CA 93729
(559) 439-7258 or (888) 439-7258

History Publishing Group materials may be purchased
for educational, business, or sales promotional use. For
information please contact: Marketing Department, History
Publishing Group, Inc. at the above address and phone
numbers.

Cover Design © Book and Cover Layout
Suzanne Moles/Wattleweb Global Solutions

Printing
Quill Driver Books/World Dancer Press, Inc.

ISBN 10: 0-9768252-1-X
ISBN 13: 978-0-9768252-1-0
LCCN 2005936415

To my wife Mary,
Who runs a beautiful home,
Manages our business affairs,
Reared two precious children,
Maintains an exciting social life,
Helps in the causes of her community,
and
Keeps a difficult husband happy.
With gratitude and love

TABLE OF CONTENTS

TABLE OF CONTENTS

TABLE OF CONTENTS

TABLE OF CONTENTS

INTRODUCTION

Is America Losing its Memory?

Who are we? What is our past? American democracy was founded upon what principles? How can we sustain them? These are questions that have perplexed us for a long, long time, and the answers still elude us to some extent. Yet the very asking of them reveals just how much Americans believe that a common understanding based upon some common knowledge of our nation's past is imperative. It draws people together. It gives us a common, civic identity. Indeed, the promise of America is premised on the need for an educated citizenry. Thomas Jefferson articulated the idea in stark terms when he said, "If a nation expects to be ignorant and free, it expects what never was and never will be."

Today a fear exists that America may be losing its memory - that our shared collective consciousness may be fading. Numerous studies have shown that even in America's best universities and colleges, many of our future leaders are graduating with an alarming ignorance of their heritage. It is almost as if we have been afflicted with a kind of historical amnesia. In this way, historical illiteracy hangs over us like a cloud. This book is offered with this in mind.

I have been a teacher for over thirty-three years. I have taught history in the sixth grade, the eighth grade, and in college. I have earned both a B.A. and an M.A. in history, and for ten years have hosted a television show during which I share historical vignettes with my audiences.

Over the years, certain stabiles have emerged in my mind regarding the teaching of history. I will resist the temptation to fix the blame for our growing historical illiteracy and will instead focus on some tactical solutions.

First we must recognize that Americans of all ages live in a "sound-bite" world. The hectic pace of today's living means that most of us have very little time for history so we skip it altogether. If only we had a tool that would teach us in smaller bites we would have time to digest the past. This book was conceived with this in mind.

Second, we must realize that any encounter with history needs an infusion of passion. All of us have our senses assaulted daily with electronic gadgetry, videos, DVDs, and the like. If the muse of history is to compete, she must spread her wares with excitement. Persuading Americans to read history is not impossible, but it takes some effort. This book was conceived with this in mind.

Third, it must be realized that the reading of history can be entertaining in and of itself. Some of the great stories of America's past can grip us and provide us with the mind altering experience of losing oneself on the back pages of the past. This book was conceived with this in mind.

This edition of Twist in Time includes seventeen fresh vignettes. The stories have been grouped into five categories, beginning with the Revolutionary War period and extending to the Twentieth Century. As a result, the reader will move with greater ease among the different eras of American History.

One final word remains. At first blush, it may seem that this book constitutes a collection of historical trivia. Nothing could be further from the truth. In composing the segments, I have attempted to set each story firmly in its broader historical context. It is true, that I have endeavored to pique the reader's interest with stories that have an unexpected ending, but this does not diminish the significance of the piece. The cast of characters, as varied as they are, and the plots, when juxtaposed with each other, reflect a unified whole.

Thus, to our readers we offer this revised edition of Twist in Time. They will see that no era of our past is immune from those strange twists of fate that shake us from our dogmatic slumbers and give us cause for reflection. From Jefferson, Adams, and Jackson, to Amelia Earhart and Adolph Hitler, our stories cover the broad spectrum of our nation's political, social, and economic past.

It is hoped that our readers will find these "Twists" both enjoyable and worthwhile.

Bill Coate
Madera, California
March 2006

TWISTS

FROM

EARLY AMERICA

Boston Massacre

The snowball fight of March 5, 1770, is a well known story. British soldiers guarding the Boston custom house fired into an unruly mob of dock workers, killing five of them. When Samuel Adams, published an account of the shootings, the episode became known as the Boston Massacre. Little did the Patriot leader know the strange chain of events that would follow his expose.

After Sam Adam's publication, the colonists were furious and demanded justice. So vociferous were they, that the British authorities decided to make scapegoats of the Redcoats.

The first to be put on trial was Captain Thomas Preston. He was found innocent. That left the eight soldiers, who now realized more than ever that they needed a good lawyer. Had their Captain been found guilty, that would have rendered them guiltless; they had just been following orders. But with

Preston having been found innocent, the soldiers were now on their own - hung out to dry. At that point, the best lawyer in Boston stepped in to take their case and save their lives.

When the trial opened, the defense attorney, who was himself a colonial, was held in almost as much ridicule as the soldiers. Cold stares surveyed him in court, and he met with outright hostility on the street. Nevertheless, he persevered.

The defense counsel maintained that the mob into which the defendants had shot, was in reality an unlawful assembly. So brilliantly did he argue the case that, after 2 1/2 hours, the jury came back with a not guilty verdict for six of the soldiers and manslaughter verdicts for the other two.

None of the defendants in the Boston Massacre went to jail. Even the two guilty ones, claiming a common law custom, escaped prison by being branded.

Thus it was that eight British Redcoats owed their lives and their freedom to a colonial lawyer who laid aside his own political feelings to do his duty. For you see, that Boston attorney who successfully defended the soldiers of the Boston Massacre was none other than John Adams, our second President, one of the most ardent anti-British patriots Massachusetts ever produced.

Benjamin Franklin

Benjamin Franklin, was one of the most astute Americans of his time, and as such, he wasn't about to allow himself to be played like a violin. He was never known to yield to manipulation. At least that became the opinion of folks in Wrentham Massachusetts, after he turned them down on their appeal for help in obtaining a church bell.

The trouble began at the end of the War for Independence when a dispute arose which divided the citizens of Wrentham. The discord grew so intense that the dissidents departed, started their own town, and named it New Wrentham.

The first building the citizens set out to erect was their own church. This was not surprising since New England tradition put that institution at the cultural, social, religious, and governmental center of every town. The founding fathers of the new community went right to work, but there was a problem. When they finished building the church, someone noted that there was no bell in the steeple.

This meant that there was no way to summon the local citizens for services, or for emergencies such as fire. Therefore, the town leaders put their heads together and came up with a plan.

Knowing of Franklin's interest in community building, the folks of New Wrentham figured they could count on him for their bell. All they needed was to gain the old patriot's attention. To accomplish this, they put a proverbial carrot at the end of the stick and announced that they had changed the name of their town to Franklin, in hopes that he would help them.

Next they wrote him a letter, informing him of their action and asking him to donate a bell for their church. Dr. Franklin, however, was not too impressed. He wrote back, suggesting that "sense is better than sound," and offered a better way for him to assist the fledgling community.

Instead of a bell, Franklin sent the good citizens a crate of books, intimating that they should forget about the house of worship for awhile and start a library. For Franklin, books were much more important than the sound of a church bell.

The people followed Franklin's advice and as a result, today, over 200 years later, they have the oldest public library in the United States - a continuing monument to Benjamin Franklin's refusal to allow any group of people to use him for their own purposes, not even when they were willing to change the name of their town.

Dr. Benjamin Church

Dr. Benjamin Church was a Boston physician who joined his fellow colonists in their vociferous objections to the actions of the British Crown during the turmoil that led to American independence. He railed against the Stamp Act and the Townsend Acts. He loudly lamented the loss of American lives at the Boston Massacre, and there is some evidence that he might even have been a participant in the Boston Tea Party. To be sure, on the surface, his patriotism could never be questioned, but little did anyone imagine just how much he enjoyed the company of ladies with loose morals or what that would cost him in the end.

All the time that Dr. Church was establishing his stellar reputation as a good family man, a competent physician, and a patriot beyond reproach, he was keeping company with a number of fast living women whose desire for the good life kept the doctor in constant financial distress. By 1775, he had to face facts. Either he would have to discard his mistresses, or he would have to find other sources of revenue. That's why he decided to approach the British.

Doctor Church agreed to betray his fellow patriots for a price. He would send enciphered messages to the British detailing the location of munitions stores, troop movements, and other military intelligence. In return he would be handsomely remunerated.

None of Church's double-dealing, however, leaked out until late in 1776. Up to that time he was held in such high esteem that he was chosen to escort George Washington into Cambridge on the day of his arrival to take command of the continental army. Later the General made him surgeon general of the army.

Doctor Church's treachery was discovered entirely by accident. One of his lady friends was caught carrying a message to him from the British. Once it had been deciphered, Church was exposed, and everyone was shocked beyond belief.

Washington hardly knew how to react, so he simply put him on trial for treason. He was found guilty and sentenced to spend the rest of his life in prison. Later he changed his mind and sent Church into exile on a ship bound for the West Indies. On the way a storm came up, and Church was lost at sea. He was never heard from again.

Some years after he died, hard evidence came to light proving that it had been Church who had alerted the British to the fact that the colonials were storing arms and ammunition at Concord. Thus his death at sea became a blessing for the countrymen he betrayed. With the doctor consigned to a watery grave, no state would have to provide a plot of ground for his remains. America's very first spy would forever be a man without a country.

Lynch mob in action

The story is old and often told. An outrage against public morals lights the fires of revenge, and lynch mobs rush in to insure satisfaction. Over the decades, thousands have been denied justice at the hands of enraged citizens who more often than not take their victims to the nearest tree and leave them dangling at the end of a rope.

Nearly everyone rejects these explosions of vigilante justice. That is why lawmakers have promulgated a number of "lynch laws" at the federal and state levels. It is just too bad that while they are at it, they can't rescue the reputation of the man whose name has become synonymous with these illegal attempts to administer justice.

The use of the term "lynch mob" has its origins in the American Revolution. After forming an army and declaring their independence, the colonies prepared to take on Great Britain, the most powerful nation in the world. At the same time, however, they had to deal with enemies within.

Not every American colonist supported the fight

for independence. About one out of four remained loyal to the king. They were called Tories, and they were generally despised with a vengeance by the rest of the population.

Actually, mob action against Tories began a good while before fighting between the Patriots and Redcoats broke out. Tory Edward Snow found his Massachusetts home befouled with feces and feathers in 1770, and again the next year. Poor old Filer Dibblee, a Tory from Connecticut, was victimized so many times that he slit his own throat, and this happened well before the Boston Tea Party.

With the actual outbreak of hostilities in 1775, Tories from Massachusetts to Georgia suffered at the hands of the Patriots. None, however, was more persistent in his persecution than a certain justice of the peace from Virginia. His stated objective was to "harry the loyalists out of the land."

One did not have to commit a crime in his neighborhood to be punished. All that was necessary was for one to be charged with being a Tory. Any person who was even suspected of being a loyalist was hauled before the magistrate and summarily deprived of land, houses, and livestock. After their appearance in court, local Patriot mobs would then plunder the Tory home and turn the booty over to the Continental army. This gave rise to the term "lynch mob," and there was a good reason for that.

The judge who opened up Tory homesteads to Patriot plunder was none other than Charles Lynch of Lynchburg, Virginia. His autocratic, legal pronouncements from the bench gave rise to the term, "lynch law." In time this was applied to any attempt by self-appointed guardians of the public good to administer justice, and there it stands today.

What began as one man's fight for patriotism during the American War for Independence, came to be known as "Judge Lynch" in action. Within a decade or two the term was being applied to any uncontrollable mob. One has to wonder what Justice Charles Lynch of Virginia would think about the legacy he left to American jurisprudence.

John Adams

The 4th of July has become one of America's most celebrated holidays. Family barbecues, homemade ice cream, and fireworks consume the nation, as its citizens pay tribute to what they consider to be the birthday of the United States. It is a grand show of patriotism, but there is one small problem. Nothing very important happened on July 4th, 1776, except that the delegates of the Constitutional Convention in Philadelphia had to cut their work short because of a horde of giant horseflies that invaded Independence Hall.

The first official move toward independence from Great Britain came on June 7, 1776, when Richard Henry Lee of Virginia petitioned the Second Continental Congress to make a clean break from the Mother Country. Nearly all of the delegates leaned toward Lee's clarion call, but few had the fortitude to take the final step that would turn the colonies into "free and independent states." They preferred to ponder the problem for awhile, so they tabled Lee's motion.

The delegates did indeed ponder the problem, but not for long. In less than a month, they experienced a remarkable change in attitude. Recent actions by the British put reconciliation beyond reach. By July 2, 1776, the colonists were ready for action, and Lee's motion for a Declaration of Independence was brought back for a vote. It passed unanimously, and Thomas Jefferson, with four other delegates, accepted the assignment to prepare the wording of the document that recorded the act of Congress.

That night John Adams wrote to his wife, Abigail, "The Second Day of July, 1776, will be the most memorable in the history of America. I am apt to believe it will be celebrated by succeeding generations as the Great Anniversary Celebration."

So just what did happen on July 4th, 1776? Actually the Congress met that day for a single item of business. They gathered to simply approve the wording of the document which had been drawn up by Jefferson and his colleagues.

As the meeting was called to order, the July temperature began to rise quickly. The sergeant at arms opened the windows to allow any hint of a breeze to flow across the room. Unfortunately, or perhaps fortunately, a slight puff of wind brought with it an invasion of giant horseflies from a nearby stable. The assembled delegates, who had been arguing over trivial points in Jefferson's wording, were suddenly swatting horseflies.

After a few minutes of battle, the insects prompted one tormented delegate to move to accept the document as it then stood. The motion was seconded and passed, as the delegates fled the building and the horseflies.

Therefore, the notion that July 4th, 1776, is Independence Day clearly misses the mark. The vote on independence had been taken two days earlier, and the document itself wasn't signed until August 2, 1776.

What Americans should be celebrating on July 4th is National Horsefly Day, for it was those pesky insects that cut short the debate on the wording of Jefferson's document and preserved its dignity for future generations.

Hamilton and Burr

The United States owes a great debt to Alexander Hamilton. As our first Secretary of the Treasury, his aggressive plans for putting the newly created United States on firm financial footing were brilliantly successful. If only he had been as assertive with a dueling pistol, he might have lived to a ripe old age.

The headstrong Hamilton was chosen by President George Washington in 1789 to solve a host of financial problems facing the young nation. Sometimes he had to step on the toes of his political adversaries, but he always did what he thought was right and was never deterred. That's why folks gave him at least an even chance when Vice-President Aaron Burr challenged Hamilton to a duel.

Burr was at the end of his term as Jefferson's Vice-President, and knowing that he would not be offered an encore, he decided to run for Governor of New York. Burr had the backing of most of the Federalists except Hamilton, who opposed the Vice-President vociferously. Soon criticism led to insults and Burr issued his challenge for satisfaction.

The two men and their seconds met on July 11, 1804, at Weehawken, New Jersey, across the Hudson River from New York City. Armed with pistols, they stepped off the required number of paces and turned to fire. Much to everyone's surprise, however, Hamilton stood holding his gun to his side. He contemptuously refused to fire while Burr took perfect aim.

The Vice-President fired and Hamilton fell, mortally wounded. Within hours he was dead, and the nation was mourning its first Secretary of the Treasury. Today most folks scratch their heads with wonder at such blatant disregard for self-preservation, but few know the real reason for Hamilton's refusal to fire. He didn't shoot because of the memory of a dead son.

You see, just two years earlier, almost to the day, Philip Hamilton, Alexander Hamilton's eldest son was killed in a duel on that very spot where his father now faced Burr, and from that day forward the Secretary vowed that he would never again fire a gun in anger. He had to show up when Burr challenged him; his honor was at stake, but he didn't have to shoot. With the image of his slain son haunting him, Alexander Hamilton chose principle over pride and lost his life.

Jonathan Edwards was a great preacher, perhaps the best the 18th century had to offer. His well known sermon, "Sinners in the Hands of an Angry God," made him famous. Reverend Edwards was a straight-laced, no-nonsense Puritan, and he raised his children to be the same. It's a real pity that his grandson didn't listen.

Edwards fathered eleven children--three sons and eight daughters, one of whom, Esther, married the President of Princeton University and gave birth to a sickly son. Twice, before he was two years old, the child narrowly escaped death, so it comes as no surprise that the daughter of Jonathan Edwards determined to see that her child was brought up in a "peculiar manner" for God.

All good intentions to the contrary, however, the grandson of the man who brought America to her knees during the Great Awakening, proved to be a "dirty, little, noisy boy who was sly and mischievous." He required a strong hand to bring him to terms.

Out of a sense of obligation to his family history, the precocious lad was induced to began the study of theology, but that didn't last long. He was soon ostracized by his Church for spreading the heresy that the road to Heaven was open to just about anyone. That's when he decided to study law.

After service in the Revolutionary War, the young man opened his law practice and began to indiscriminately court the girls, most of whom he promised to marry. These activities put a strain on his pocket book, and soon he was facing a debtors' prison, so he turned to politics. By 1800, he had become the Vice-President of the United States, and he might have become the Nation's Chief Executive if he hadn't killed a former Secretary of the Treasury in a senseless duel.

He escaped a murder trial, but later became involved in yet another scandal which resulted in his being accused of treason - and by now you've guessed the identity of this child gone astray. His name was Aaron Burr, the man who shot Alexander Hamilton and tried to incite an insurrection in Mississippi and Louisiana. Burr died in 1836, and one has to wonder what Jonathon Edwards, his Puritan grandfather would have said at the funeral of his grandson who seemed to have gone out of his way to "shake his puny fist in the face of an angry God."

Aaron Burr

Light Horse Harry Lee

Robert Morris could have been a hero in American history, if he hadn't tried so hard to line his own pockets. When his fiscal bubble finally burst, he was thrown into jail, but even that wouldn't have been so bad, if only he hadn't taken a real hero down with him.

At the peak of his career, Robert Morris financed the American Revolutionary War on credit. He cornered the tobacco market, and controlled a vast empire in banking and shipping. No doubt about it, he was a brilliant tycoon, until he dreamed up that scheme for building a large town along the banks of the Potomac River.

At first blush, it looked like the perfect plan. The land could be had for a pittance, a town developed, and then lots sold at a price that would yield astronomical profits. All he needed was some additional capital, and that's why he went to

Light Horse Harry Lee, the father of General Robert E. Lee.

Lee invested his family fortune in the scheme and then sat back to reap the reward - he didn't have to wait long. Come to find out, the land titles could not be cleared because of a technicality, and the whole plan went belly up. Morris and Lee both went to jail.

It was a sad spectacle, especially for Lee - the man who had been such a brilliant general in the Revolutionary War, the man who had been the Governor of Virginia, the man who as a member of Congress had stood up and eulogized George Washington as "first in war, first in peace, and first in the hearts of his countrymen" - sitting in a debtor's prison.

In 1800 Congress passed the Bankruptcy Act, which allowed Morris and Lee to be set free. The former died shortly thereafter, but Lee lived on to suffer continued humiliation at home. Finally he abandoned his family and left for the West Indies, in a solitary attempt to recover his fortunes. It was futile.

In 1818, Lee decided to return home but never made it. On the return voyage he was stricken with typhoid fever and died. He was buried by the ship's crew on Cumberland Island, Georgia. Thus Light Horse Harry Lee, with his reputation in shreds, became the final casualty in that wild speculation of Robert Morris.

Robert Morris

James Madison

Washington D.C. is an awe inspiring place. Visitors are struck with the majesty of the city on the Potomac. Little do they know that had it not been for some shenanigans at a dinner party in 1790, The hub of government might have been located somewhere else.

It all began on the morning of July 20, 1790. Secretary of State Thomas Jefferson had come upon a dejected Secretary of the Treasury, Alexander Hamilton, waiting to see the President. Hamilton was despondent because he couldn't persuade Congress to pass his plan for putting the newly created United States on firm financial footing. The obstacle was James Madison, a leader in the House of Representatives, and Hamilton was so frustrated that he was on the verge of tendering his resignation to President Washington.

Although he was not a political ally of Hamilton's, Jefferson did recognize the need for a sound financial policy, so he offered to mediate the deadlock between Madison and

Hamilton. Jefferson offered to host a private dinner party where the two antagonists could meet alone to see if their differences might melt away under the more benign influences of wine and gentlemanly conversation.

Not surprisingly, it was Jefferson who opened the subject, and Madison responded. He objected to the Federal government taking over the Revolutionary War debt of the individual states. His home state of Virginia had already paid off its obligations, while most of the northern states hadn't paid a penny.

At that point, Jefferson unleashed a stroke of genius. The assumption of state debts would be much more palatable to the South if the permanent capital of the nation were to be placed in Virginia. Madison was all ears; indeed, this would stifle much of the southern criticism.

And so it happened. Madison withdrew his adamant opposition to Hamilton's funding bill, and it passed. In its next legislative breath, Congress passed the Residency bill, which placed the nation's capital at its present location on the Potomac.

Thus it was that both the financial fate of the United States and the site of the seat of government were settled at a simple dinner party. As a result we now send our representatives to Washington D.C. instead of Philadelphia or New York, proving once again that politics is the art of the possible.

Benjamin Franklin

Everybody knows that Benjamin Franklin left this nation quite a legacy. His inventions, his diplomacy, and his plain old common sense are still admired today. There was, however, one bequest that wasn't appreciated by all of Franklin's contemporaries, and it landed his grandson in jail.

As he approached the end of his long life, Benjamin Franklin sat down to write his last will and testament. He all but passed over his son, William, not because he was illegitimate, but because the younger Franklin and his father were on opposite sides during the War for Independence and became bitter enemies.

Instead, Benjamin bequeathed almost his entire estate to his daughter Sara Bache, and to her son, Benjamin Bache, Franklin left his printing press.

Benjamin Franklin Bache, the grandson of Benjamin Franklin took possession of the press at the death of his grandfather. He started his own newspaper, and by the late 1790s he had become well known for his caustic commentaries about the administration of President John Adams.

That would have been all well and good, except that it

was against the law. In 1798, Congress had passed the Alien and Sedition Acts which, among other things, made it a crime to criticize the government in print.

It should have come as no surprise that the grandson of Benjamin Franklin would not be throttled by this egregious attack upon the freedom of the press. He immediately began to publicly attack the administration's foreign and domestic policies. This, of course brought Bache into direct violation of the Sedition Act, and he was thrown into prison.

Two years later, Thomas Jefferson replaced Adams as President, and he pardoned all those convicted under the Sedition Act. Sadly, this did not free Bache from prison. He had died behind bars just a few months before. Apparently the grandson of Benjamin Franklin had inherited from his grandfather, not only the means to propagate great ideas, but the will to stand by them as well.

Thomas Jefferson

Thomas Jefferson, author of the Declaration of Independence, Washington's Secretary of State, and third President of the United States was not above criticism. In 1802, his political enemies decided to get personal by accusing him of having an affair with Sally Hemings, one of his slaves. Recently, scientists and historians have discovered considerable support for the allegation, but there is another piece to the story that is being ignored, and it involves Jefferson's wife.

Martha Wayles was born at "The Forest," her father's plantation near Williamsburg, Virginia. She was married early to a Mr. Skeleton, but at the age of 22 was widowed. In 1771, she remarried, this time to Thomas Jefferson, the "Sage of Monticello," where she went to live.

Like many of the Tidewater planters, John Wayles was a large slaveholder, and when he died, Martha Jefferson inherited 135 slaves, all of whom came to Monticello, and among that group was little Sally Hemings.

As time went on, Jefferson and Martha became the parents of several children, one of whom was named Mary. Young Sally Hemings became the child's handmaiden and assumed even more responsibility for her after Martha died in 1782.

In fact, while Jefferson was minister to France in the early days of the Republic, he brought Mary and Sally with him. By then Sally was fifteen years old and moving into womanhood. It was during that sojourn in France that Jefferson is alleged to have first become intimate with Sally.

Once they were back home, Jefferson apparently continued his dalliance with Sally and fathered several children by her. By the time he was President, the secret was out, and tongues began to wag. Jefferson neither confirmed nor denied the rumors, and life went on at Monticello as usual.

In 1826, Jefferson died, and in accordance with an agreement that he had made with Martha Jefferson before her death, he gave Sally Hemings her freedom, for you see, not only was Sally the consort of Jefferson; she was his wife's half sister as well. John Wayles, Martha's father, was also Sally Hemings' father by one of his slaves, Elizabeth Hemings.

So the story of Thomas Jefferson and Sally Hemings has continued for 200 years, but their full relationship has been hardly understood. When Jefferson decided to make Sally his concubine, he was simply choosing his sister-in-law. Apparently miscegenation in early America was a family affair.

Thomas Jefferson

Epitaphs can be very insightful. One can wander through a cemetery and learn history right from the tombstones, and if the epitaph was composed by the one who lies beneath the marker, the graveyard visitor becomes privy to the private thoughts of the departed as well as an accounting of his life on earth. This is what Thomas Jefferson had in mind when he wrote his own epitaph, but when people read it, they were more than a little surprised.

When Jefferson retired from public life, he went to his beloved Monticello to live out his days. Most of the time he read, wrote letters, and tinkered, but as he drew close to the end, he gave serious thought to his grave and to the tombstone that would mark it.

It didn't take Jefferson long to decide where he wanted to be buried. He would lie in repose right there at Monticello. Nor did he labor long over the grave marker. It would be a simple stone obelisk. With these matters settled, Jefferson then turned to the inscription that would be chiseled into the granite. How did he want to be remembered by the American people?

Surely he would want his tombstone to reflect that he was the third President of the United States. From 1801 to 1809 he had guided the Ship of State through perilous times, and most assuredly this represented the apex of his service to his country.

By the same token, certainly he would have the monument maker engrave that he had been Vice-President of the United States. From 1797 to 1801, he had served under President John Adams with whom he had many differences. That in itself would be worthy of inclusion in his epitaph.

Then there was the fact that he had been the nation's first Secretary of State, under President George Washington. This signal honor was sure to find a place in his epitaph.

In addition, Jefferson had been U.S. Minister to France and the Governor of Virginia. What man could leave these accomplishments off his tombstone?

Thomas Jefferson died on July 4th, 1826, and was buried at Monticello, according to his wishes. When his tombstone was unveiled and his epitaph revealed, the country found out just how important, or rather how unimportant, Jefferson's political life had been to him.

The inscription was simple. It read:

Here was Buried
Thomas Jefferson,
Author of the Declaration of American Independence, of the
Statute of Virginia for Religious Liberty, and Father of the
University of Virginia.

His political life paled into insignificance when compared to his creative genius that found its expression in independence, religious liberty, and education. Those are the things for which Thomas Jefferson wanted to be remembered. That is why there isn't a word in his epitaph about being President, Vice-President, or a diplomat.

Battle of New Orleans

The date was January 8th, 1815, and the British army had assembled eight thousand battle-seasoned troops on the outskirts of New Orleans. They were facing a hodge-podge force of Americans led by Andrew Jackson. The British sacrificed two thousand men that day, but by a quirk of fate, it was all so unnecessary.

The War of 1812 easily ranks as America's worst-fought war. The disunited country couldn't even defend its own capital, as the British put Washington D.C. to the torch and ran President James Madison into the nearby hills.

It is not surprising then that the British became a bit overconfident as they assembled just below New Orleans to attack the motley crew which General Andrew Jackson called his army.

On January 8, 1815, Sir Edward Pakenham led his redcoats in a frontal attack against the Americans. Awaiting his adversary's advance was Jackson with a polyglot collection of Tennesseans, Kentuckians, Creoles, and pirates drawn up behind breastworks. For all their drill and bravery, the lobster backs advancing through the open were no match for Jackson's well protected men. Making good use of artillery as well as rifles, the Americans held their fire as each wave of attackers approached, then sent deadly volleys at close range. Finally the British retreated while an American band struck up "Hail Columbia" and sang this popular little ditty, "Behind it stood our little force - None wished it to be greater; For every man was half a horse, and half an alligator."

Left behind were seven hundred dead, including Pakenham himself, fourteen hundred wounded, and five hundred prisoners. Jackson's losses were confined to eight killed and thirteen wounded. Clearly the British lion's tail had been twisted, but it had all been for naught.

Two weeks earlier, on December 24, 1814, the peace treaty between the United States and Great Britain had been signed. The opposing forces in the Battle of New Orleans had no idea that the War of 1812 was over before that first shot was ever fired.

Thomas Jefferson and John Adams

Thomas Jefferson and John Adams may have been political enemies, but their lives were really not all that different. They were co-authors of the Declaration of Independence. They both were elected President of the United States, and with more than a touch of irony, the two men faced the Grim Reaper in an amazing coincidence.

When the people of the United States chose George Washington in the nation's first presidential election in 1789, they also installed John Adams as Vice-President. Washington then appointed Thomas Jefferson as his first Secretary of State, setting the stage for a political fight that would carry on for a decade or more.

Although Jefferson and Adams had stood side by side against King George III, after independence was won, they drifted apart politically. Jefferson was much more democratic, while Adams kept his aristocratic New England bearings. Such was the cleavage between them that when Washington declined a third term in 1796, Jefferson ran against Adams and lost.

By 1800, Adams was all set for a second term, but Jefferson campaigned hard against him. He charged that while

Adams sided with the rich folks, he, Jefferson, stood for the common man. It was an effective argument, given Adams' natural propensity towards aloofness, and when the votes were finally counted, Jefferson won.

Adams went back home to nurse his political wounds in Massachusetts, while Jefferson went to the nation's new capital, Washington, D.C. He served two terms and then retired to his beloved Monticello in Virginia.

Although they never did completely reconcile their differences, in later years the two old patriots did manage to sheath their political swords to some extent. They engaged in a mutually respectful correspondence for years, and one would have thought that they had effected a complete rapprochement. Then the 93 year-old Adams became ill in the summer of 1826 and died.

However, before America's second President breathed his last, he whispered in words that had just a tinge of lament, "Thomas Jefferson survives." Adams left this world thinking that his old adversary had won the final battle—longevity-- but he was wrong.

For you see, Thomas Jefferson joined John Adams in death that very day, July 4th 1826, exactly fifty years after the approval of the Declaration of Independence. However, the Sage of Monticello left this earth first. In an ironic twist in time, Adams won the final victory; he outlasted Jefferson by five hours, but he never knew it.

Twists

from the

Civil War

Brooks Assaulting Charles Sumner

Members of the Congress of the United States have a number of privileges, not the least of which is the right to say just about what ever they please on the floor of the Senate or the House. They can't be sued, and historically there has been little to restrain their rhetoric, except for that time when terseness was forced on one Senator with a club.

Charles Sumner came to the Senate from Massachusetts just before the Civil War. He was what we would today call a "dandy." Brilliant, learned, handsome, articulate, he had made a name for himself as a reformer, especially an anti-slavery reformer.

In the spring of 1856, Sumner, believing he could launch into a tirade with complete abandon, took a nasty swipe at the proponents of slavery, and in so doing made some vicious attacks on Senators Stephen A. Douglas and Andrew P. Butler. Although Butler was absent, Douglas heard it all and muttered, "That darned fool is going to get himself killed by some other darned fool." Indeed, that "fool" materialized in the person of Congressman Preston Brooks, a nephew of Senator Butler.

For a few hours, Brooks thought about challenging Sumner to a duel. Then he decided that he could reflect his contempt more effectively with a cane. Two days after Sumner made his comments from what he thought was the safe harbor of the Senate floor, Congressman Brooks entered the chambers as it adjourned. While Sumner remained at his desk writing, Brooks approached his kinsman's critic, cane in hand.

Before anyone knew what was happening, Brooks was raining blows down upon the head of Senator Sumner, who fell to the floor "bellowing like a calf."

As disreputable as it was, Brooks showed that no one spoke with complete immunity on the floor of Congress. That caning took Charles Sumner out of the Senate and shut him up for three years.

And it made no difference that the House censured Brooks. He resigned, returned home, and was triumphantly reelected. In the meantime the representatives of the people learned a lesson; freedom of speech is not absolute and certainly not without its consequences - not even on the floor of the United States Senate.

Throughout the course of our nation's legal history, temporary insanity has been an often used, but seldom successful, defense for murder. American juries generally have been very reluctant to accept this explanation for violent action, notwithstanding the fact that the first time it was used, it set a member of Congress free after he had taken the life of a famous American.

In February of 1859, Daniel E. Sickles, who was in Washington D.C. representing his New York constituents in Congress, was shattered by the news that his wife had been holding amorous rendezvous with his best friend in a rented apartment.

The friend, who came from a highly respected and well-known family, was the U. S. Attorney for Washington D.C. He was known to be a ladies man, but had aroused no suspicions in Sickles' mind, until he was apprised of the illicit liaison by an anonymous informant.

When Sickles confronted his wife, Theresa, with the allegation, she broke down and confessed. The equally distraught husband demanded a written confession from his wife and then sent her packing to her mother's. That left him to deal freely with Philip Barton Key, the man who had defiled his bed.

On Sunday, February 27, Sickles, while looking out across Lafayette Square from his window, spied Key walking up Pennsylvania Avenue. Enraged, he grabbed his pistol and stormed out of the house to confront his adversary.

Sickles caught up with Key almost within the shadows of the White House and put a bullet in him at point blank range. Key died there right on the street, and Congressman Sickles was arrested.

During Sickles' trial, he offered a novel defense for the time - temporary insanity. The court pondered it, and the jury bought it. Congressman Daniel E. Sickles was set free, and a celebration, which included most of the jury, was held in a nearby hotel.

Public sentiment gushed forth in support of the innocent verdict. Society would have no truck with scoundrels who trifled with the domestic relations of another man's home, not even when the defiler was the son of Francis Scott Key, author of the Star Spangled Banner. Apparently when the "Dawn's early light" revealed Philip Barton Key's dishonorable advances, The mental "rockets red glare" that ignited Sickles' passion was enough to convince a jury for the first time that temporary insanity made the killing justifiable.

Daniel Edgar Sickles

President James Buchanan

The American Civil War began under the administration of Abraham Lincoln, or so the history books tell us. We have been taught that the first shots of that terrible conflict were fired on April 12, 1861, when the North attempted to reinforce Fort Sumter in Charleston Harbor. A closer look, however, raises some doubts as to precisely when the War began, and who was President at the time.

With the election of Abraham Lincoln in 1860, South Carolina seceded from the Union and was soon followed by six other Southern States. The fat was in the fire, but it was President James Buchanan who had to cook it, not Abraham Lincoln. The President-elect wouldn't take office until March.

Buchanan would have loved to just let things simmer until the inauguration of the new President, but he was backed into a corner. The recently occupied garrison of Ft. Sumter was badly in need of supplies.

So, in early January, he ordered the Star of the West, a merchant ship, to deliver the much needed provisions. Down the coast it went to Charleston. On January 9, it reached its destination. Unfortunately South Carolina was ready.

Buchanan's Secretary of State, John Floyd, a southern sympathizer, had warned the Rebel authorities that the Star of the West was on its way, and a battery of anxious cadets from the Citadel positioned several guns at the shore. When the supply ship entered the harbor they let loose with the first shots of the Civil War, three of which hit the Star of the West.

With that, the Star retreated to open waters and returned to its home port. She had been driven off by hostile fire, but as we said the fat was in the fire.

When Lincoln was sworn in, one of his first acts was to re-order the provisioning of Ft. Sumter. This second attempt was likewise repelled by the Rebels, and there was no turning back. The War may have begun in earnest on April 12, 1861, but the first shots over Ft. Sumter were fired months before, while James Buchanan, not Abraham Lincoln, occupied the White House.

In 1861, the Confederate Army fired on Fort Sumter in Charleston Harbor. As fate would have it, the enemy commanders were well acquainted with one another, and this fact had fatal consequences for a certain private, Donald Hough.

Before the Rebels began their attack on Fort Sumter, General P.G.T. Beauregard sent a message out to Major Anderson, his old artillery instructor at West Point. The Confederate General, sure that he was going to be successful in taking the fort, informed Anderson that when the inevitable occurred, the Union commander would be given the opportunity to salute the Stars and Stripes before it was replaced with the Stars and Bars. With this understanding between the two former comrades, the ball began.

The Confederate batteries opened fire first, while Anderson and his troops remained sheltered in the covered casements, unable to do little damage to the Confederate gun positions. Finally, when it became obvious to everyone that the fort was going to fall, Anderson signaled his intention to surrender, but before he did, he was going to take advantage of his past relationship with his adversary.

So Anderson ordered his guns to make ready for the salute which Beauregard had promised. Halfway through the observance, however, one heavy gun exploded and killed Private Donald Hough instantly.

During that siege of Fort Sumter, not one soldier lost his life, but in this one act of military courtesy extended by Beauregard to Anderson as he was surrendering his position, Donald Hough was accidentally killed by "friendly fire" and became the first man to die in a war that would see the deaths of more than 600,000 other men and boys. In retrospect, it seems a pity, at least for Hough, that his commanding officer was on such friendly terms with the enemy.

Colonel Elmer Ellsworth

Symbols - they can make one swell with pride - or wretch in disgust. Take that flap about flying the Confederate flag above the state house in South Carolina for instance. That may have been the most recent fight over that symbol, but it won't be the last, and it certainly wasn't the first.

The guns had barely quieted at Fort Sumter when President Lincoln ordered that Alexandria, Virginia, just across the Potomac, be taken from Rebel hands. After all, there staring him in the face each morning was the Confederate flag flying from atop the Marshall House, and he wanted it taken down.

The soldier who was placed in charge of this detail was Colonel Elmer Ellsworth, one of the four soldiers who formed the President's body guard. Ellsworth's orders were simple. Take the town and remove that flag. The former was easy, but the latter had its price.

Ellsworth's troops landed early on the morning of May 24, 1861. There was no resistance, so the Colonel marched directly to the Marshall House where the offending bit of bunting waved in the breeze. Flanked by a quartet of soldiers, Ellsworth climbed to the second story of the hotel unmolested.

From one of the top windows he clambered out onto the roof and cut the flag from its staff. With the emblem in hand, Ellsworth then made his way back to the stairs from which he intended to descend and make secure his occupation of Alexandria.

He had no more than reached the top step when from out of the shadows lurched an enraged Rebel who would not stand for such an abominable sacrilege as the desecration of the Confederate flag. He raised a gun to Ellsworth's heart and fired, killing him instantly. Needless to say the assassin was quickly dispatched as well.

They brought Ellsworth to Washington where Lincoln mourned the fallen soldier calling him the "greatest little man I ever met." In the meantime, the Confederate flag never went back up on the Marshall House, but it flew in thousands of other places, and as recent events show, it still stirs the emotions of partisans, almost 140 years after that first forced removal of the stars and bars.

The McClean House at Bull Run

The American Civil War was a watershed in our nation's history. It redefined the character of the United States and sent the population of the South reeling, especially people like Wilmer McClean who always seemed to be in the wrong place at the wrong time.

Wilmer McClean was one of the more prosperous residents of Manassas Junction, Virginia, in July of 1861, when the Northern and Southern armies began to gather around his place. His 1,400 acre plantation straddled Bull Run, so the Confederates occupied his house and used it as its headquarters in this, the first real, full-fledged battle of the Civil War.

After the First Battle of Bull Run, McClean sold his farm and moved further west, out of the line of fire between the two contending armies. He assured his family, "the sounds of battle would never again reach them" in their new home.

In the meantime, battle followed battle,

Chancellorsville, Fredericksburg, Gettysburg, Vicksburg, and hundreds of others. For four years Billy Yank and Johnny Reb pounded each other, and as they did, they got closer and closer to Wilmer McClean's new home.

Finally in April, of 1865, Lee's Army of Northern Virginia and Grant's Army of the Potomac faced each other, and where do you think they were? Somehow the center of this horrific conflict, which began at his Bull Run farm four years earlier, had sought McClean out and found him once more. The Union and Rebel forces were camped once again, almost in his front yard.

On April 9, 1865, General Robert E. Lee surrendered to Ulysses S. Grant, and since they were so close, the combatants took over McClean's home once again - to agree upon and sign the terms of the capitulation. When he left his home on Bull Run to find that safe haven from the ravages of war, McClean settled near Appomattox Courthouse never dreaming that he was jumping from the frying pan into the fire.

The McClean House at Appomattox

General Benjamin F. Butler

Resistance to what Southerners called the War of Northern Aggression took many forms. In addition to armed conflict, the citizens of the South stood ready to show their contempt for the Union army in ways that were almost as vexatious as drawn swords, especially down in New Orleans.

By the summer of 1862, the Union Navy, under Admiral David G. Farragut had made possible the occupation of New Orleans by General Benjamin F. Butler, who in addition to holding the city, announced his determination to force its citizens to bend their knees to his occupying forces. Unfortunately for the general, that was easier said than done.

While Union soldiers were apparently safe to walk the streets of New Orleans, their flag could not go unattended. On June 7, 1862, one fellow by the name of Mumford decided to haul down the stars and stripes and cut the flag of the United States up into lapel stickers. This was too much for the General. He ordered Mumford executed.

If Butler thought, however, that a hanging would elicit better manners from the Confederates, he was mistaken. Now it was the women's turn. The Southern belles developed the habit of congregating on the hotel balconies dressed in all of their fineries. Whenever a Yankee soldier passed by, they would all whirl around and flirt out their skirts, causing one officer to comment that "Those women evidently know which end of them looks the best."

The greatest insult to northern dignity, however, was yet to come. On one occasion Admiral Farragut himself, while walking to a dinner engagement, passed beneath the balcony of a hotel. Suddenly he was drenched in a downpour from above. Several women had emptied the contents of the hotel's slop jars directly on the heads of the Admiral and his party.

Butler was livid and issued his famous General Order Number 28 which said that any female showing contempt for the United States, shall be held liable to be treated as a woman of the night.

Butler always claimed that General Order 28 put an end to such loathsome expressions of contempt, but it was also noted that while performing patrol duty, the Union soldiers did so from the middle of the streets. They no longer seemed willing to subject themselves to the possibility of a vengeance from above, which often reeked to high heaven.

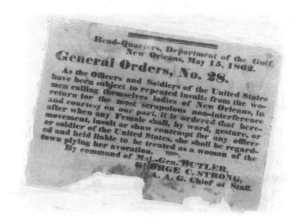

Gen. John Morgan

The sanctity of womanhood - every Southern male was taught to respect it, and when the Yankees invaded their homeland during the Civil War, they fought for it almost as fiercely as they did to keep slavery. Then along came Captain John Dowdy. On Christmas Day, 1864, one woman put him to the test, and all of his fine upbringing couldn't save her life.

Captain Dowdy rode with Morgan's Raiders. He and his comrades raised such havoc in Tennessee and Kentucky that a $1,000 bounty was put on their heads. On September 4, 1864, Dowdy was encamped with the rest of the troopers about two miles outside of Greenville, Tennessee. General John Hunt Morgan was headquartered in Greenville proper, at the Williams home. He thought he was safe there, but he had reckoned without Mrs. Williams, who had dollar signs in her eyes.

Captain Dowdy rode in to the Williams home at 4 o'clock in the morning to receive orders from the General for troop movements that day. Morgan sent a directive to the troops to be ready to move by 7 A.M. Dowdy saluted smartly and took his leave. He never saw his commander again.

At 6 o'clock over eighty Yankees came out of nowhere and surrounded the Williams home. The General grabbed his pants and boots and ran, still in his night clothes, into the garden to hide, but it was futile. His betrayer, Mrs. Williams, yelled out, "There he goes," pointing to the shrubbery in which

Morgan had secreted himself. His pursuers quickly found him and put several bullets into his chest.

Meanwhile, the camp was also attacked, and Captain Dowdy was captured and taken to an Ohio prison. He remained a prisoner of war for almost four months and then managed to escape. After crossing the Ohio River, the Captain rode through Kentucky and Tennessee. He was headed back to Greenville to settle a score.

On December 25, 1864, Captain Dowdy arrived at the Williams home. He didn't have to go to the house; he spotted Mrs. Williams coming up from the cow pen. With his arms folded, Dowdy blocked the path.

"Oh Captain Dowdy," a stunned Mrs. Williams exclaimed. Dowdy responded with a terse, "Correct Ma'm."

Sensing that she was in trouble, the woman cried out, "Captain, don't kill me. I'll give you the thousand dollars." Dowdy calmly replied, "If you have anything to say, you have five minutes to talk."

The shaken woman dropped to her knees, preferring at that point to address the Almighty. When the five minutes expired, so did Mrs. Williams. Captain Dowdy shot her at point blank range, killing her instantly. He picked her up and carried her to the front porch. After crossing her hands, he rode off without looking back.

Notwithstanding the fact that Captain Dowdy shot an unarmed woman in cold blood, Chivalry in the South remained alive for many years thereafter. Women continued to be the objects of manly affections and respect, except for those rare instances when circumstances, such as Captain Dowdy faced, tore the mantle of virtue off the fairer sex, and they came tumbling down from their pedestal to a more level playing field.

Johnny Clem

In 1932, a dottering old man dressed in an old army uniform asked for quiet. A crowd of well-wishers had gathered to celebrate his 80th birthday. Everybody present, including the press, referred to him as Major John L. Clem, but he wanted to be remembered as "the Drummer Boy of Shiloh."

Johnny Clem was one of the youngest soldiers of the Civil War. He was just ten years old when he served as a drummer boy for the 22nd Michigan Infantry.

The soldiers of Johnny's unit saw a little action in 1861, but it wasn't until the Battle of Shiloh in early April of 1862, that they received their baptism by fire, and it just so happened that the young drummer boy got caught right in the middle.

On April 6, Johnny's unit was caught off guard and was

almost pushed into the Tennessee River. During the fighting a Union soldier dropped right at his feet, nailed by a sharpshooter. Ten year-old Johnny picked up the dead man's rifle and drew a bead on a Rebel Colonel who had failed to see the small lad with the big gun. In the next instant, the Confederate officer was on the ground. Johnny Clem had killed him with one shot.

The Battle of Shiloh lasted two days and up to that time was the bloodiest conflagration that had ever been fought on the American continent. The North lost 13,000 men, while the South counted 10,700 casualties.

An account of the Battle of Shiloh of course made the newspapers, and in every piece, the story of Johnny Clem's bravery was told. Soon the entire nation knew about him.

Johnny ended the war as a teen age Sergeant and sported a medal given to him by the Secretary of the Treasury. He remained in the army and retired at the age of 65 with the rank of Major. When Clem died at the age of 82, his military tombstone was inscribed with the usual information: name, regiment, company and state, but in Johnny's case it also carried an epitaph, "Here lies the Drummer Boy of Shiloh." Now no one would forget.

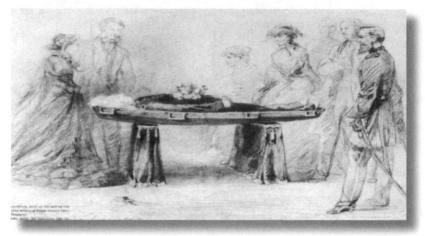

Edward D. Baker

Edward D. Baker was a one-time Illinois lawyer and an intimate friend of Abraham Lincoln. He went west during the California gold rush and wound up in Oregon in 1860, where he was elected to the United States Senate.

When the Civil War broke out, no one was more pro Union than Senator Baker. "I want a sudden, bold, forward, determined war," he proclaimed after the firing on Fort Sumter. So intent was he on punishing the South that he joined the army as a Colonel while holding on to his seat in the Senate.

Colonel/Senator Edward Baker divided his time between the army and the Senate. From time to time he would return from the field, appearing in full uniform on the floor of the Senate where he would unbuckle his sword, lay it across his desktop and launch into an oratorical attack upon those of his fellow lawmakers who appeared to favor any compromise with secession.

Then on October 21, 1861, he took leave of his Senate desk to lead his regiment up Ball's Bluff, on the Potomac. His task was to cross the river and disperse the Confederate snipers who fired at will from the brush and timber atop the Bluff. There was no doubt in Baker's mind that his troops would carry the day. He reckoned, however, without the tenacity of the Mississippi and Virginia soldiers who commanded the Bluff.

For the Rebels it was a turkey shoot. Panic quickly ran through the Union ranks, and in short order they were frantically sliding back down the Bluff and heading toward the Maryland side. As telegraphic accounts of the rout reached the President, both he and Congress awaited the fiery report from Baker that was sure to come, but this was not to be. Baker had taken to the Senate floor for his last time. His body lay back up on the Bluffs, the victim of the deadly snipers fire that took 200 other lives.

Thus the senator who had so dramatically prodded his fellow legislators while adorned in his military garb, had fallen victim to his own rhetoric. It was one thing to harangue the halls of Congress in favor of military action. It was quite another thing to put one's own words into action. As a senator and a soldier, Edward Baker did both and paid for it with his life.

The Ruins of the Henry House

By all accounts, the American Civil War was the bloodiest conflict the United States has ever endured. More than 600,000 soldiers died, and this figure does not take into account the toll on the civilian population. Numerous stories of non-combatants abound, and of these, none is more poignant than that of Judith Henry.

In July of 1861, Mrs. Henry and her boys found themselves the unwilling pawns in the first real battle of the Civil War. They lived just two or three miles northwest of Manassas Junction, which was itself just 20 miles south of Washington D.C. For days the Confederate forces had been assembling around the hill upon which the Henry house sat. The family knew that it was just a matter of time until the Union army would challenge the right of a Southern army to camp so close to the nation's capital.

On July 21, 1861, the fight began, and the Henry home was caught right in the middle. With muskets popping and artillery shells exploding, Mrs. Henry's sons prepared a litter for their mother and evacuated the house. They carried her to the shelter of a nearby ravine. There they saw war at its worst.

Soon both armies were contending ferociously for control of Henry Hill, and the fighting disintegrated into hand-to-hand skirmishes. It was more than Judith Henry could take.

Amidst the smoke and groans of battle, Mrs. Henry asked that they leave the protection of the ravine and return to the house. When her sons hesitated, she insisted. She begged so piteously to be allowed to die in her own bed that they relented and brought her back, and there she had her wish. A shell hit the bedroom and killed them all the instant they laid her down. As the house began to flame, her lifeless body was riddled with bullets.

At the end of the day, silhouetted against the smoke filled horizon and flanked by torn and tattered trees were the ruins of the Henry House - all that remained of a lifetime of labor brought to an end by the horror of war.

Judith Henry was probably never counted in any wartime statistic, but she paid the ultimate price just as if she were a soldier in battle - with one huge difference. Unlike Billy Yank and Johnny Reb, she at least was able to die in her own bed.

When hostilities at Fort Sumter launched the nation's gruesome Civil War, the young man from Canton, Massachusetts, decided to answer Lincoln's desperate call for volunteers. He joined the Union Army, and in a short time he was helping to guard Washington D.C., a job he took seriously; after all, he had quite a family name to uphold.

On October 21, 1861, his regiment was ordered to Ball's Bluff, just a short way up the Potomac. His job was to rid the area of the concentration of Rebel soldiers that were threatening the capital. He shouldered his rifle with joy; after all, he had quite a family name to uphold.

He engaged the enemy that day and along with 700 other infantrymen, was captured. They marched him to Libby Prison in Richmond, and there they kept him as a prisoner of war. He bore the indignity with honor; after all, he had his family name to uphold.

Then came the order from President Jefferson Davis that some of the prisoners at Libby Prison were to be executed in retaliation for the proposed hanging of a crew of privateers caught in an attempt to run the Yankee blockade. The young soldier drew one of the short straws and prepared to meet his maker, but he did so stoically. After all, he had quite a family name to uphold.

Just as he was on the verge of mounting the scaffold, the soldier received a reprieve. President Lincoln had canceled the hanging of the privateers, so President Davis followed suit with a pardon of his own. Within weeks, the soldier was exchanged and returned to his regiment. His war was a long way from being over, though. After all, there was that family name he had to uphold.

The young soldier fought valiantly during the Peninsula Campaign, at 2nd Bull Run, and Antietam. Then they marched him to Gettysburg. He was helping the wounded after the first bloody day on that battlefield when he was shot in the head and died instantly. Now he wouldn't have to worry about upholding that family name any longer. He had performed after a manner that would have pleased his grandfather. Paul Joseph Revere, Jr., the grandson of that other Paul Revere of the Midnight Ride fame, had acquitted himself admirably. Now he could rest in peace, with his family honor in tact.

Paul Revere's Midnight Ride

John Rowlands

One of the most peculiar aspects of the Civil War era is the fact that its landscape was crowded with figures who were marked for later fame. Generally, these individuals were cast in minor roles in the conflict itself, but they certainly made their entrances on the stage of world history in the years that followed. Take Private John Rowlands, for instance.

Rowlands was a member of the 6th Arkansas Infantry. He was just twenty years old on that April Sunday in 1862, which could help explain his actions during the bloody battle of Shiloh.

Confederate infantrymen stormed the last center of Federal resistance on the first day of the battle, and Rowlands was there. He had come up from Cypress Bend with the "Dixie Greys." When the darkness silenced the musket fire, Rowlands and his Confederate comrades were much relieved. On the next day, however, it was a different story. The Northern army regrouped and pushed back. In the confusion that followed, Rowlands was captured.

As he was about to be herded back to a Yankee prison, Private Rowlands had a sudden change of heart. He indicated that he now realized that he had been on the wrong side all along. He wanted to switch sides and join the Union Army! And that's what he did.

It wasn't long, however, before marching under the Union blue got the best of Rowlands, so he reported himself ill and was dismissed on account of poor health. Now he was faced with a dilemma. He couldn't remain with the army, and he couldn't go home, so he came up with another idea. He joined the Union Navy.

Rowlands served in the Navy until the end of the War, and when he wasn't immediately discharged, he deserted that branch of the service.

All told, his was a pretty dismal service record. He had been a turncoat, a malingerer, and a deserter. Maybe that's what later propelled him to action in a far off continent - Africa. For you see, in time John Rowlands changed his name to Henry M. Stanley, and it was he, this failure as a soldier and a sailor, who searched for and found Dr. David Livingstone in 1871, and uttered that now famous line, "Dr. Livingstone, I presume?" Who would have ever guessed?

"Taps" on the Battlefield

The Civil War, although moving further and further into our nation's past, has left a legacy of heartache and heroism which affects us today. We are still moved by those stories of brothers fighting brothers and fathers fighting sons. One such tragedy occurred in 1862, during the Peninsula Campaign, but unlike so many others, this sacrifice had eternal consequences. It left a piece of the soul of the entire nation that can still be heard wafting across cemeteries today.

It all began at Harrison's Landing, Virginia, in the aftermath of battle. A certain Union Captain by the name of Ellicombe and his men stumbled upon the bodies of several Confederate soldiers. Ellicombe ordered his men to bury them, and as they were doing so, he surveyed the faces of the young men who had been cut down in the flower of youth. Suddenly, to his horror, he spied the face of one he knew; it was that of his own son.

Part of Ellicombe's shock stemmed from the fact that he had not known that his son had joined any army, much less the Confederate army. The boy had been studying music in the South when the war began. After hostilities broke out, communications broke down, but Ellicombe assumed that his son would be safe as long as he continued his study of music. Unfortunately for the younger Ellicombe, such was not the case. The boy left school to join the Confederate forces.

Captain Ellicombe tenderly searched his son's pockets, and among his personal items he found a scrap of paper with some music written on it. He handed it to his bugler and asked him if he could play the tune. When the bugler said he could, the Captain asked for and received permission to give his son a special burial. As the lad was consigned to the grave, the bugler played the musical notes that had been scribbled on the piece of paper carried by young Ellicombe.

The sound of the music as it drifted across the countryside that morning sent chills up the spines of everyone within ear sound, including Captain Ellicombe's Division Commander, General Daniel Butterfield. When he heard the music, the General inquired of his Captain, whence came the notes? Ellicombe gave Butterfield the paper that had been retrieved from his son's pocket.

The General had it copied and then gave it to his own bugler, Oliver Morton, and ordered him to prepare a new bugle call from the Ellicombe music. It was such a beautiful melody and so simple that it caught on quickly among other buglers. Before the war was over, buglers on both sides were playing the piece at graveside ceremonies.

By some strange twist of fate, the notes of that scribbled song carried by a schoolboy in the American Civil War went on to become the bugle call for funerals around the world. Today we call the music "Taps," and it is still being played, especially for military services, for it signals the end of a soldier's struggle, as he is laid to rest.

General Stonewall Jackson

It's no secret that General Stonewall Jackson had some strange ideas about health matters. Some historians have even called this great Civil War General a hypochondriac and insist that, had it not been for his unusual beliefs, he might not have died from that wound he received at the Battle of Chancellorsville.

Although he was one of the most talented field commanders in American history, Jackson thought of himself as "out of balance," and even under fire in battle, he was given to raising one arm in order that the blood would flow down his body and establish equilibrium.

As for his diet, he refused to eat pepper on the grounds

that it made his left leg weak. He often sucked on lemons, believing that they cured his "dyspepsia," and his staff knew that even on the march, he would want his raspberries, bread, and milk for medicinal purposes.

The General was comfortable only when in a bolt upright position, with his organs held "naturally," one atop another. That's why he spent hours standing up while reading the Bible.

Jackson's list of physical complaints was as long as his arm. He imagined that he suffered from rheumatism, chilblains, neuralgia, biliousness, and a distortion of the spine. None of this, however, would have made any difference if only he hadn't insisted upon treating his own ailments.

To rid himself of nearsightedness, Jackson often dipped his head into a basin of cold water, eyes wide open, for as long as he could hold his breath. On other occasions he attempted to relieve all types of pain by applying ice cold towels to his body, and it was this last procedure that cost him his life.

After he was wounded by his own men at Chancellorsville, surgeons had to amputate one of his arms, and while he was recovering, one of his servants applied the General's usual remedy for pain. Without the knowledge of attending physicians, they placed the cold towels on Jackson's body. Within hours he contracted pleurisy and pneumonia and died.

So the South lost one of its greatest generals, and Robert E. Lee lost his right hand man. The eccentricities of the old soldier which had won him such acclaim on the battlefield finally turned against him, proving once again that "he who doctors himself has a fool for a patient."

General Lee and Stonewall Jackson

In May of 1863, the Union commander, General Meade with 130,000 men, faced Confederate General Lee and his 60,000 men, along a line south of the Rappahannock River in the vicinity of Chancellorsville, Virginia. Although Lee was badly outnumbered, he did have an advantage. He had Stonewall Jackson - at least for a little while.

Facing heavy odds, Lee took a chance. He sent Jackson with 26,000 men, on a fake retreat. Meade thought for sure he had the Rebels on the run. He was, however, sadly mistaken.

At 5:30, on May 2, Jackson suddenly turned and came out of the woods into which he had retreated. He fell upon the right flank of the Union army and sent them reeling. Then the two armies licked their wounds and prepared for the next day.

On May 3, 1863, the Battle of Chancellorsville was intense. Artillery roared. Muskets fired, and soldiers fell by the hundreds. As night approached, Jackson, accompanied by members of his staff, undertook a reconnaissance of the enemy.

The General started out down a plank road toward the Union lines, but before he did, he gave his pickets an explicit order. Shoot any one who comes up that plank road, and ask NO questions. The soldiers listened all too well and ultimately obeyed.

Presently Jackson came upon a force of Yankee infantrymen and was forced to turn and skedaddle back along that same plank road, down which he had ridden, apparently forgetting the strict orders he had given his own skirmishers.

As Stonewall approached the Confederate lines, a flash of flame lit the scene for an instant, and within that space of time, in a moment of irony, the South was deprived of one of its greatest military leaders. General Thomas "Stonewall" Jackson had been mortally wounded by his own men, who were simply following their leader's orders.

With Jackson's death, Lee was never quite the same. To have lost his general to a Yankee bullet or artillery shell, would have been one thing, but to lose him to friendly fire was incomprehensible. One has to wonder how things would have turned out if only Jackson had been a bit more cautious in returning to his own lines on that fateful night when he was dispatched by his own soldiers.

Vicksburg, Mississippi

Historical truth can be an elusive thing, especially when it comes to some of those Civil War stories. One such case is that of the minie-ball pregnancy, and we want to advise our readers right here at the start that their credulity is going to be stretched just a bit before this one is over.

In the November 7, 1874, issue of the American Medical Weekly is an article written by a Dr. L. G. Capers Jr. entitled "Notes from the Diary of a Field and Hospital Surgeon, C.S.A."

According to Dr. Capers, On May 12, 1863, he beheld a young comrade fall suddenly to the ground. The medic ran to offer aid and found a compound fracture of the left tibia caused by a minie-ball which had then ricocheted from there upward through the man's body and out his groin.

As the Dr. dressed the wounds of the poor fellow, a woman came running from the porch of a nearby house. One of her daughters also had been wounded. Hastening to treat the young lady, Capers found that she too had received a minie-ball wound. It had penetrated the left abdominal region. Dr. Capers did what he could, but then had to retreat. After the battle, Capers was able to visit the young woman frequently, and just 278 days from the date of the receipt of the wound by the minie-ball, he "delivered this same young lady of a fine boy, weighing 8 pounds."

About three weeks after the birth, Dr. Capers was called to examine the baby and extracted a mashed and battered minie-ball from the child.

At that point, the doctor claims to have solved a mystery. He wrote, "The ball I took from the babe was the identical one which, on the 12th of May, shattered the tibia of the young soldier, and in its mutilated condition, plunged through his groin, and into the left ovary and the uterus of the girl, impregnating her!"

Now as for the truth of this story, your guess is as good as ours. However, as they point out in a Vicksburg, Mississippi museum, if it is true, we suppose that makes the little baby the world's one and only, honest to goodness "son-of-a-gun."

Daniel Edgar Sickles

Daniel Edgar Sickles lived most of his life in the public eye. While representing New York State in the United States Congress in 1859, he shot and killed his wife's paramour almost within the shadows of the White House. When the victim turned out to be the United States Attorney for Washington D.C., Sickles made headlines in almost every newspaper in the country.

Although the shooting was deemed "justifiable homicide," most pundits considered Sickles to have committed political suicide. But that was before his Civil War maneuvering rescued his reputation.

When the War Between the States broke out, Sickles raised a New York regiment and was made a Brigadier General. By the time of the Battle of Chancellorsville he had been promoted to Major General and given command of the Third Corps of the Army of the Potomac. That was his position on that fateful day of July 2, 1863, during the second day of fighting at the Battle of Gettysburg.

Still commanding the Third Corps, Sickles in violation

of orders, advanced on the Union Forces at the Wheat Field of Gettysburg, stretching his lines too thin and inviting an attack by the Confederates under General Longstreet. The Third Corps was plain lucky that day, but Sickles was not. A cannon ball hit his leg and it had to be amputated. Sickles' war was over.

Determined to fend off severe public criticism of his impulsive movements on July 2, Sickles ordered that his leg be preserved and sent to Washington D.C. There he accompanied it to a medical museum, thereby showing the mesmerized media the sacrifice he had made for his country. After the war, Sickles made several trips to the Washington Museum to visit his own leg, each time building considerable public sympathy. As a result, he was made Ambassador to Spain and then once more was elected to Congress. In 1895 he authored the bill creating the Gettysburg National Park.

In 1914 Daniel Sickles died and was given a hero's burial in Arlington National Cemetery. His masterful job of spin control, using his own leg, had rescued him from any serious alienation of national affection.

Daniel Edgar Sickles after Amputation

William Harvey Carney

William Harvey Carney was born in Norfolk, Virginia, in 1840 and attended a school for Blacks which was conducted secretly by a local minister. When the Civil War broke out, Carney made his way to Massachusetts and in time joined the famed Morgan's Guard, which became part of the 54th Massachusetts Infantry Regiment. It was while he was thus engaged in the service of his country that Carney etched an indelible mark for himself in our nation's history.

It was in July of 1863 that Carney found himself engaged in the disastrous battle at Fort Wagner. His regiment was part of a large force whose task it was to storm the sandy beaches of Morris Island, South Carolina and take Fort Wagner. As William and his comrades inched toward the Confederate defenses, the minie balls took their toll, as did the Rebel artillery. Carney was hit twice, but still he moved inexorably toward the enemy. He was determined not to stop until he reached the Rebel ramparts, then he spied the flag.

Carney saw the color bearer receive a hit. It was a stomach wound, but somehow the soldier held on for a moment. William, who was bleeding himself, reached the mortally wounded soldier as he slumped to the sand. Carney made a dive for the flag. He grabbed Old Glory just before it too hit the ground.

Somehow throughout the remainder of the battle, Carney miraculously held on to the American flag and kept it aloft. 1,757 Union soldiers were killed or wounded on the sands before Fort Wagner, and bleeding from his own wounds, Sergeant Carney worked his way to his regimental commander and presented him with the Stars and Stripes. "The old flag never touched the ground," Carney whispered before he fell to the ground unconscious from the loss of blood.

Sergeant William H. Carney recovered from his wounds and in later years was in great demand as a leader of Memorial Day parades and as a speaker at patriotic events. For you see, this refugee from the South, this hero of the 54th Massachusetts Infantry, this African-American who was willing to lay down his life to save the flag, was the first Black soldier in the history of the United States to receive the Congressional Medal of Honor.

General Earl Van Dorn

During the Civil War, it wasn't just the privates who died; sometimes the generals gave their lives as well. Consider Albert Sydney Johnston, Stonewall Jackson, or JEB Stuart. They all fell in defense of the South in battle and were mourned by their fellow Confederates. Then along came General Earl Van Dorn. He was shot all right, but not on the battlefield.

Van Dorn was a West Point graduate and career soldier. When the War between the States broke out, he resigned his commission and joined the Confederate Army and was quickly made a general.

His service for the Confederacy was something of a mixed bag. He enjoyed military successes in Texas and in the early defense of Vicksburg, but came out the loser in the Battle of Pea Ridge and at Corinth. Then he found his niche in the cavalry and scored a stunning victory at Holly Springs. Suddenly Van Dorn was a hero and Jefferson Davis gave him a corps and ordered him to middle Tennessee.

As fate would have it, Van Dorn established his

headquarters at the home of one Dr. Aaron White in Spring Hill, Tennessee. Now it just so happened that the other physician in town, Dr. George Peters, who was away serving in the Tennessee State Legislature, had left his beautiful wife Jessie, who was 24 years his junior, at home alone. Somehow Jessie made General Van Dorn's acquaintance and soon was making regular visits to his headquarters. So violently did tongues wag that Van Dorn had to move his headquarters to Martin Cheair's mansion, but it was all to no avail. Everywhere that Earl went, Jesse was sure to follow.

Well, it was just a matter of time until Dr. Peters came home and learned of the alienation of his affections by Van Dorn. Therefore, on May 7, 1863, as the General sat as his desk, Dr. Peters calmly walked past the guards, entered the house and shot Van Dorn in the head from behind. The general lived about four hours and then gave up the ghost.

It seems ironic that Van Dorn would meet such an inglorious end. If only he had heeded an earlier warning from another woman in another town. "Let the women alone until the war is over." Van Dorn replied, "I cannot do that, for it is all I am fighting for." One gets the feeling that perhaps he was talking about more than just preserving the honor of southern womanhood.

The Sultana, a Mississippi River boat

War often brings out the worst and the best in people. Heroes, cowards, and villains all have played their parts in our nation's conflicts - especially the Civil War. A prime example can be seen in the case of the Sultana, a Mississippi River boat whose greedy captain caused the death of hundreds of Union soldiers.

It was in the dark of the early morning when the Sultana steamed north on the Mississippi River. It had picked up its passengers at Vicksburg and was headed north carrying more than 2,000 men. They had survived the horrors of Confederate prisons and had been paroled. Now they were going home, or so they thought.

Unfortunately, back in Vicksburg the Captain, in an effort to squeeze every dollar he could out of the run, had packed paying civilian customers onto the deck of the ship along with his military consignment of passengers. The overloaded boat pressed on, passing Memphis and continued steaming north until it had gone about 90 miles. Suddenly the boilers exploded. The strain had been just too much. The vessel literally blew apart.

As fate would have it, the levees on both sides of the Mississippi had been so demolished that all of the surrounding bottom lands were flooded to a width of 50 miles. Now more than 2,000 bodies bobbed in that water.

Of that group, 1900 soldiers perished that morning. Corpses were found as far south as Helena, Arkansas. It was America's worst-ever maritime disaster, and it was fraught with irony.

Most of those soldiers had been in Southern prisons for two years or more. After lengthy negotiations they had been repatriated. Families were preparing for their return home. But this was not to be. One greedy Captain and an overworked boiler did what sharp-shooters and prison guards could not.

On April 27, 1865; 18 days AFTER Lee surrendered, the soldiers on the Sultana died with hardly any notice, and that's the clincher. To die in battle is one thing; to die needlessly after the last bullet has been fired is quite another.

Edmund Ruffin

The Confederate States of America had no more fervent advocate than Edmund Ruffin. The man was loyal to the bone. So widely known was his patriotism that he was given the honor of firing the first shot of the Civil War, never dreaming that he was lighting the fuse of his own demise.

If Southern thought and action could be represented in a single individual, then Edmund Ruffin would be the most likely candidate. Born in the early days of the Republic, Ruffin was a Virginia farmer whose experiments in soil chemistry markedly improved the productivity of Southern agriculture. He became widely known for his writings on farm subjects, and then used this bully pulpit to preach the doctrines of slavery, states' rights, and secession.

By 1861, Ruffin had come to hate the North with every ounce of his sixty-seven-year-old body. He admitted to having prayed on his knees that Lincoln might be elected so that it would bring on a war for Southern independence.

In December of 1860, when South Carolina held its Secession Convention, Edmund Ruffin was given the seat of honor. In the weeks that followed, he saw his picture sold all over Charleston, as the wave of Rebel patriotism began to swell toward its violent climax.

When the moment of decision finally came, Ruffin was made a temporary gun captain and led to the shore batteries that faced Fort Sumter. There he fired the cannon shot that started the Civil War. Six days later he was made an honorary member of the Palmetto Guard and even donned a Confederate uniform. Then he hobbled home to await the outcome of the struggle.

Four years later, Lee surrendered to Grant. The War was over, and no Rebel was any more disillusioned than Edmund Ruffin. So distraught was the 71 year-old that he armed himself and prepared to take aim once more. This time however, he turned the gun on himself. In one final act of defiance, the man who fired the first shot of the Civil War ended his own life rather than endure what he was sure would be the ravages of Yankee domination.

President Abraham Lincoln

President Abraham Lincoln is perhaps the most revered of all American Presidents, and no small portion of this adulation has emerged from his image as the Great Emancipator. "Lincoln freed the slaves" is the household understanding of the man, but a second look at his famous Emancipation Proclamation raises a big question mark.

Lincoln issued the Emancipation Proclamation on January 1, 1863. With the stroke of a pen, the President transformed the Civil War into a struggle for human freedom. Lincoln's order freed all of the slaves within any state or part thereof that was in rebellion against the United States of America.

Thus it was that human bondage was outlawed in most of the states of the South. Later generations extolled the virtue of this edict, but as a practical matter, it DIDN'T FREE A SINGLE SLAVE!

In the first place, the Emancipation Proclamation did nothing to eliminate the peculiar institution in Missouri, Kentucky, Maryland, or Delaware. Those slave states were loyal to the Union and unaffected by the Proclamation.

Likewise 13 parishes or counties in Louisiana and the entire state of Tennessee were exempt because by 1863, they were no longer in rebellion. West Virginia, which had seceded from Virginia was, in the words of the document, "left precisely as if this proclamation were not issued."

So it was, that in reality, Abraham Lincoln's Emancipation Proclamation freed not one single slave. In the slave states which were not in rebellion - where Lincoln could have freed the slaves - he didn't, and in those Confederate states and portions thereof which continued by force of arms to resist the Federal government - where he had no coercive power to free the slaves, he ineffectually proclaimed their freedom. In other words, the status quo prevailed.

Of course slavery was finally outlawed in the United States, but it took the 13th Amendment to the Constitution to accomplish it. The Proclamation of the Great Emancipator fell on deaf ears as long as brothers continued to kill brothers on the battlefields of the Civil War.

Slavery in the South

Mary E. Surratt

The United States was ablaze with fury. An unthinkable conspiracy had unfolded; cowardly killers had struck! People braced for the worst, including germ warfare and poisoned water supplies. Clearly the President had to do something, so he came up with the idea of a military tribunal to try the culprits.

Although these chilling words may have a modern ring to them, they actually describe another crisis our country was facing almost a century and a half ago, and they were the prelude to a judgment that has been debated ever since.

President Abraham Lincoln was hardly cold in his tomb when President Johnson determined not to allow those accused of conspiring to kill him to stand trial in a civilian court. Instead they were compelled by executive order to face a military commission.

A hue and cry arose from some circles as to the legality of such a move. Counsel for the defense claimed that the military had no jurisdiction over civilians, and thus such a trial would be unconstitutional, but in the end it all fell on deaf ears. The President had his way, and eight persons were tried for murder and conspiracy to commit murder.

The military panel, composed of 9 army officers, began hearing testimony on Friday, May 12, 1865. More than 350 witnesses took the stand, and over the next six weeks a wide range of topics found their way into the official transcripts. There was talk of attempts to poison New York City's water supply and to infect clothing with yellow fever and smallpox. In the end, however, it was the assassination of President Lincoln and the attempt upon the life of Secretary of State Seward that sealed the fate of the co-conspirators. Eight were found guilty, and half were sentenced to die. The other four received prison sentences of varying lengths.

On July 7, 1865, the four condemned prisoners were led to the gallows. The knees of one had to be bound for modesty's sake, for she was a woman, Mary E. Surratt. Within minutes the quartet dropped into eternity. Not only had the military tribunal avenged the assassination of President Lincoln, it had made history by ordering the first execution of a woman in the United States of America.

The hanging of Mary E. Surratt

Caricature of a Carpetbagger

After the Civil War, the states of the former Confederacy were inundated with a special breed of opportunists whom the Southerners labeled Carpetbaggers. These unwelcome visitors were viewed as interlopers who shoved their snouts in the public troughs of old Dixie and drained them dry. By in large, they were a much despised bunch, all except for one woman from Maine. When she arrived in Williamsburg, Virginia, with her carpetbag, it didn't take folks long to see that she had only come for what belonged to her.

The woman's story had its beginning during the first days of the Civil War. The Confederates had just fallen back from Williamsburg leaving, not only their own dead and wounded, but those of the Union army as well. The good women of Williamsburg then went out onto the battlefield to tend to the dying. That is how Kate Rowland met the soldier from Maine.

The mortally wounded Yankee had no hope of recovery, but he was conscious to the end. As Kate tried to make him as comfortable as possible, he extracted a solemn promise from her. He wanted his grave to be well marked and his wife told of its whereabouts. "I know she will want to come for me, if she can find my grave, and move me home." The soldier soon expired, and Kate did as she was told. She marked his grave well and sent a letter to his widow.

The war closed, and several years later the soldier's widow wrote Kate that she was coming to claim her husband's remains. When she arrived in Williamsburg, Kate accompanied her to the grave. She could not help but notice, with a touch of irony, that the widow carried a carpetbag.

As they stood at the grave, the widow indicated her desire to dig him up, so she hired some nearby workers to do the job. Down, down, down went the spades until they struck the broken, crumbling remains of a coffin in which lay the skeleton of the poor soldier.

At that point, the widow shocked Kate to her toes. She ordered the workers to lift her husband's remains and put them in her carpetbag. "You men just double him up and put him in here," she said in an officious tone. So the skeleton was doubled up and stowed away in the carpet bag.

The Virginia lady, struck dumb as she was, silently walked by the widow's side, carpetbag in hand, to the railroad station. As she took her seat in the train, the widow called out cheerfully, "Good-bye!" Then she dumped her spouse down on the floor beside her and waited for the train to pull out.

As Kate Rowland returned to her home, she could barely wait to tell her story. Her encounter with the widow from Maine had given new meaning to a widely used epithet. Not every carpetbagger was a scoundrel. At least one had come with good intentions.

Stars and Bars

The Rebels may have lost the Civil War, but "Dixie" is still being played, and the Confederate battle flags are still flying down South - way, way down South - like in South America.

That's right, the Stars and Bars are still flying in Brazil today as the result of an emigration of thousands of Southern expatriates who journeyed there shortly after their loss in the War of the Rebellion.

Under the leadership of Confederate Colonel William Hutchinson Norris, the Southerners went into self-imposed exile after the War and established a colony called Americana. There they continued their southern way of life, including the preservation of their peculiar institution, slavery, which was not abolished in Brazil until 1888.

The Southern style plantations prospered, and soon a second and third generation of Confederados, as they came to be known in Brazil, replaced those first immigrants. In time nature had its way, and the children and grandchildren of the Southern expatriates intermarried with the general population.

Today thousands of descendants of the Confederados can be found throughout Brazil, and once a year, they gather to render homage to their Rebel roots.

First they gather at the secluded cemetery in Americana to pay their respects to their southern ancestors. Then they have a party complete with deep-fried chicken and biscuits, corn bread, and candied apples.

There's lots of Dixieland jazz, Southern Belle skirts, and lots of jokes, mostly at the expense of the Yankees. These Brazilian partygoers have names like Jones and Pyle and Steagall, but they all speak Portuguese.

And of course there is the Confederate battle flag. It's everywhere during the fiesta - in the plaza, along the streets, and even painted on the road.

That flag which has caused so much turmoil in the United States, seems not to be mired in controversy in Brazil. Quite the contrary. The Brazilian descendants of the Confederados seem to go out of their way to be seen with it.

So while the South lost the war, it seems that a part of its culture is still very much alive in Brazil, where the descendants of Confederate soldiers love to celebrate their Southern heritage, complete no doubt with an ample supply of mint juleps.

Twists

from the

White House

Warren G. Harding

Today's elections, it seems, cannot be conducted without spasms of vigorous mudslinging. Nearly everybody complains about the negative campaign tactics that always manage to cloud the issues. It's enough to make the modern voter cast a jaundiced eye toward the system - until one considers the past.

Personal attacks in political campaigns are nothing new. History has recorded some vitriolic exchanges that would make today's public disparagements sound almost genteel. Consider for a moment the campaign of 1860. Four candidates had their hats in the ring: Abraham Lincoln, Stephen A. Douglas, John Bell, and John C. Breckinridge. The four men fought like cats and dogs, and the campaign reached its nadir when Lincoln's opponents began to make fun of his looks. Lincoln's handlers rejoined by asserting, "We know Old Abe does not look very handsome, but if all the ugly men in the U.S. vote for him, he will surely be elected."

Then there was the election of 1884. Grover Cleveland was running against James G. Blaine, but he had a problem, and the Blaine people took full advantage of it. Cleveland was the father of a child born out of wedlock. Blaine said that he didn't believe that voters would "knowingly elect to the Presidency a coarse debauchee who would bring his harlots with him to Washington."

Now if that isn't enough, let's go to 1920 when Warren G. Harding was running against James Cox and Eugene Debs. This time it was the Socialist candidate who got off the best zinger of the campaign. Never known for his intellectual depth, Harding was accused by Debs of being stupid. His opponent, Debs charged, discussed the issues by "uttering pompous phrases that moved over the landscape in search of an idea."

It was the election of 1936, however, that brought out the worst in the political operatives. Stunned by Franklin Roosevelt's victory four years earlier, Alf Landon's campaign manager was quoted as saying that "If the President became convinced on Tuesday that coming out for cannibalism would get him the votes he needed, he would begin fattening a missionary in the White House backyard come Wednesday."

So the next time that civility seems to be slipping away from our political process, it might help to remember that our forefathers weren't the most magnanimous campaigners who ever hit the trail.

Jefferson Davis

General Zachary Taylor was a proud man, and he wanted the very best for his family, especially his daughter, Knox Taylor. From her father's vantage point, no one was good enough for the young woman, not even the young lieutenant who sought her hand. "Young Love," however, prevailed and it cost the young bride her life.

In 1835, when a romance developed between his young subordinate and his daughter, Old Rough and Ready put his foot down. There was no way he would give his blessing to the match. He knew the strain that Army life put on a marriage.

At first the Lieutenant's southern pride was ruffled, and he contemplated challenging Taylor to a duel. Instead, he resigned his commission and married the 16 year-old girl anyway. Seeking refuge from the wrath of his father-in-law, the groom then took his bride to Hurricane, his plantation home on the Mississippi River.

Living life as the wife of a Southern aristocrat at first agreed with Knox Taylor. She managed the "big house," while her husband saw to the details of his first cotton crop. Everything was coming up roses, and then suddenly both husband and wife came down with swamp fever. Within three months, she was dead.

The grief stricken husband went into seclusion for more than a decade, but when the Mexican/American War broke out, he took command of a volunteer regiment, the Mississippi Rifles, and who do you think was his commanding General? Yes, you guessed it, his former father-in law, Zachary Taylor.

The two men gave each other a wide berth, until the Battle of Buena Vista, when troops led by the young officer defeated the Mexican Cavalry and saved the day for Taylor. After the dust settled, General Taylor sought out the hero of the battle. The two men eyed each other, and Taylor, offered these words to the younger man: "Sir, my daughter was a better judge of men than I was." With that they parted and continued to travel down different roads. General Taylor became President of the United States, while his former son-in-law, the man who stole his daughter away, Jefferson Davis, became President of the Confederate States of America. One has to wonder how history might have been changed if only 16 year-old Knox Taylor Davis had survived.

Tecumseh and the Prophet

It is a widely accepted belief among historians that, in describing the past, what people THINK happened is just as important as what really DID happen. No where is this more obvious than in the curse the Prophet placed on the occupants of the White House.

The Prophet together with his twin brother, Tecumseh, were Indian leaders who created a great deal of mischief for the United States Government in that area north of the Ohio River during the early 1800s. So irritating were their exploits that General William Henry Harrison was sent to pacify the Indian brothers and their followers. This he accomplished at the Battle of Tippicanoe, but not before the Prophet pronounced a curse on Harrison.

Nothing much was thought of the Prophet's curse until Harrison was elected President of the United States in the election of 1840. In March of 1841, the 69 year old Indian fighter gave his inaugural speech in a pouring rain, caught pneumonia and died after one month in office. It was at that point that somebody recalled the curse of the Prophet, eyebrows were raised, and speculation ran rampant.

Then when Abraham Lincoln was assassinated, someone remembered the Prophet's curse and noticed something that the two fallen Presidents had in common. They both were elected in a year ending in 0. And when James A. Garfield, elected in 1880, was shot, the curse of the Prophet was given wider credence. What could be more obvious? Fate was decreeing that every President who was elected in a year ending in zero must die in office, and thus it was that every twenty years the curse of the Prophet was renewed. William McKinley, elected in 1900, died in office. Warren Harding, elected in 1920, died in office. Franklin Roosevelt, elected in 1940, died in office. John F. Kennedy, elected in 1960, died in office.

Then came Ronald Reagan, elected in 1980. Would the curse of the Prophet hold true; a lot of folks thought so when he was shot. But Reagan pulled through, thus putting an end to, if not the curse of the prophet, at least the 140 year old macabre belief that a series of strange coincidences were somehow dictated by fate.

President Andrew Jackson

President Andrew Jackson was known as "Old Hickory." He was as tough as nails, and when he set out to do something, it was usually accomplished. No one ever really doubted that he would someday fulfill his promise to represent the "common man" in the White House, but neither did anyone ever expect his constituency to respond as it did when he was finally elected.

Andrew Jackson's affinity for the common man probably stems from his early life. As a youth, "Mischievous" Andy displayed much more interest in brawling and cockfighting than in his scanty opportunities for reading and writing. His grammar was always rough-hewn, and his spelling was unique. On more than one occasion, he misspelled the same word two different ways in the same letter!

As a young adult, Jackson lived by the dictum of the common man, "Give no insult, and take none." In one of his many brawls, the soon-to-be President of the United States bit the ear off of one of his opponents. There was no doubt about it, Andrew Jackson was made of the stuff the common man admired.

Then came the election of 1828. Jackson's opponent was the crusty, imperious, New England Puritan, John Quincy Adams. It was hardly a contest. The common man prevailed, and Jackson prepared to go to the White House, but on the way a funny thing happened.

On Inauguration day, "Hickoryites" poured into Washington, and characteristically, Jackson embraced them. A milling crowd of clerks, shopkeepers, hobnailed artisans, and grimy laborers were invited to the White House after the ceremony. When Jackson ordered the doors opened to the mob, they surged in, wrecking the china, climbing with muddy boots on the furniture, and threatening their hero with cracked ribs.

To lure Jackson's exuberant supporters out of the White House, tubs of lemonade and whiskey were set out on the front lawn. This of course did the trick, and the doors were quickly locked.

As for Jackson, he was spirited out a side door, and ironically spent his first night as President in a hotel room, thanks to the advent of the age of the common man.

President Andrew Jackson

President Andrew Jackson was a bare-knuckled brawler in more ways than one. He always stood his ground against his opponents, whether it was on the streets of Nashville or on Capitol Hill. He was not above rolling in the mud in a street fight, leveling a pistol in a duel, or impaling his enemies on the point of a political spear.

It is not surprising then to learn that Jackson was the first American President to become the target of an assassination. The attack occurred on January 30, 1835. Jackson was on Capitol Hill to attend the funeral services for Congressman Warren R. Davis. As the President filed past the casket and descended to the rotunda, Richard Lawrence, an unemployed house painter, stepped up, drew a pistol, and fired point blank at the former General.

A percussion cap exploded, but a bullet failed to discharge from the gun barrel. Characteristically, Jackson charged his would-be killer with complete abandon and contempt, while his breathless Vice-President, Martin Van Buren looked on, horrified.

Lifting his cane above his head, the 67 year-old Jackson lunged at his assailant. Before he could reach him, however, Lawrence drew a second pistol and fired again. Unbelievably, this gun also failed to fire.

After the second attempt failed and some semblance of order was restored, Jackson went about his business as if nothing had ever happened. As for Lawrence, he spent the rest of his life in Washington's Government Hospital for the Insane.

And Vice-President Van Buren? He gave the near tragedy considerable thought. Folks didn't call him the "Red Fox" for nothing. From that day on, Martin Van Buren never came to Capitol Hill unprepared. As the President of the Senate, he was obligated to preside over the proceedings of that body, but he didn't have to expose himself to unnecessary risks. For the remainder of his term as Vice President, Van Buren never took his place on the floor of the Senate without two pistols on his person.

Andrew Jackson may have been the first U.S. President to draw an assassin's aim, but Martin Van Buren had the distinction of becoming the first pistol-packing presiding officer of the United States Senate.

Chief Justice John Marshall

The United States has endured many Constitutional crises, but none with the poignancy of the hanging of old Corn Tassel. When this Cherokee Indian was put to death for the murder of a fellow tribesman in 1830, it set President Andrew Jackson against the United States Supreme Court and for a time put the Constitutional system of checks and balances in danger.

Corn Tassel was a member of the Cherokee tribe, located in northwestern Georgia. His people had created a state within a state, complete with a written constitution. While the United States recognized the Cherokee Nation, the state of

Georgia did not. It passed a law in 1828, declaring that all Cherokee statutes were null and void.

Therefore, when in 1830, Corn Tassel, in a fit of rage, shot one of his neighbors, Georgia authorities arrested him over the objections of the Tribal Council and prepared to put him on trial.

Corn Tassel appealed to the United States Supreme Court on the basis that the crime for which he was arrested took place, not in Georgia, but within the accepted boundaries of the Cherokee Nation.

Chief Justice John Marshall, having already ruled that the Cherokee Nation was a viable political entity, declared that the action of the sheriff in Georgia was unconstitutional. He ordered Corn Tassel to be returned to the Cherokee elders.

At that point, President Andrew Jackson intervened in the dispute by assuming jurisdiction. He had wanted for a long time to move all of the Indians west of the Mississippi River and into the Indian Territory, a place which would one day become Oklahoma.

Jackson sent federal marshals to Georgia to enforce his policy, and when reminded that the United States Supreme Court had ruled contrary to that position, the President responded, "Well, Chief Justice Marshall has made his decision. Now let him enforce it."

That, of course, did it for poor old Corn Tassel and his tribe. Georgia hanged him and destroyed the independence of the Cherokee Nation, while the Supreme Court looked on helplessly. For the first time in the Constitutional history of the Republic, the Executive Branch went nose to nose with the Judiciary, and the Judge blinked.

John Tyler

Julia Gardiner was born with the proverbial silver spoon in her mouth. She was the daughter of Juliana and David Gardiner, a prominent and wealthy New York family. From her earliest childhood, she was trained to live in polite society and made her debut at the age of fifteen. For almost a decade, she enjoyed a charmed life. Then tragedy struck and she married the President of the United States.

In 1844, after a tour of Europe, Julia's parents decided to introduce her to Washington D.C.'s winter social season. With a steady stream of soirees, the young woman became the "undisputed darling of the capital," and one of her most ardent admirers was President John Tyler.

Now Tyler had been a widower for a year and a half, and with a respectable mourning time having elapsed, he began to entertain thoughts of another matrimonial union. When the Gardiners joined the social circuit, Julia immediately caught his eye, but there was a problem. The lass was thirty years younger than the President, and her father looked with a rather baleful eye at his daughter marrying an old man. That's when President Tyler decided to make use of his office.

It just so happened that at the time the newly constructed U.S.S. Princeton was causing a stir among politicians and military men. The innovative warship was being touted as the answer to any navel threat to the United States, and President John Tyler was anxious to show her off.

Therefore on February 29, The Princeton headed up the Potomac River with a host of dignitaries aboard. Included in the group were Secretary of State Upshur, Secretary of the Navy Gilmer, Senator Thomas Hart Benton, and Commodore Robert F. Stockton. Among those also invited aboard were none other than Julia Gardiner and her father, David. Obviously Tyler had something on his mind besides naval affairs.

Halfway through the cruise, it was decided to fire one of the guns, and that turned out to be a mistake for several of the guests. For some reason, it exploded and killed eight people, including the Secretary of State, the Secretary of the Navy, and David Gardiner.

Julia, of course, was heart broken, so the President moved in to console her. Since he no longer had the opposition of her father, he invited her to the White House and continued to comfort her. So soothing were his words, that 54 year-old John Tyler convinced 24 year-old Julia Gardiner to be his wife. They were married on June 26, 1844, less than four months after the Princeton disaster.

John Tyler has not gone down in American History as our greatest President. In fact he is often referred to as "His Accidency," alluding to the fact that he ascended to the office only upon the unexpected death of President William Henry Harrison. Be that as it may, one thing is for certain. Tyler knew how to use the office - specially in matters of love.

The Presidential Seal of the United States

Throughout the history of the United States, a handful of men have ascended to the Presidency without being elected to that office. John Tyler, Millard Fillmore, Chester Arthur, and Gerald Ford, all occupied the White House without the consent of the governed.

This fact, however, has not kept our unelected Presidents out of the history books, with one noteworthy exception. In 1849, David Rice Atchinson became the 12th President of the United States, but today, hardly anyone remembers his name.

James Knox Polk had just finished a pivotal one term as President. Under his expansionist policies, the boundaries of the United States spread from the Atlantic to the Pacific, and Polk announced that he was satisfied. He would not seek a second term.

This set the stage for the election of 1848. The Whigs nominated "Old Rough and Ready," General Zachary Taylor, while the Democrats choose Lewis Cass. It really wasn't much of a contest. Taylor the hero of the Mexican/American War, won handily, and prepared to take over the reins of government in March, 1849. There were, however, just two small problems.

In the first place, March 4, 1849, Inauguration Day, fell on a Sunday. In the second place, the President-Elect was a very religious man. As a strict Episcopalian, Taylor refused to conduct any business on Sunday, and that included being sworn in as President.

Therefore, at noon on March 4, 1849, the terms of office for James Knox Polk and his Vice President, George Dallas, ended without their successors taking the oath of office. America would have been without a President had it not been for the Constitutional provision that allowed the Speaker of the House to be elevated to the Presidency in the absence of a President or Vice-President. That is how David Rice Atchinson ascended to the Presidency at Noon on March 4, 1849.

Speaker Atchinson's Presidency lasted for just 24 hours. On Monday, March 5, 1849, General Taylor took the oath of office, and Atchinson quickly became a has-been. Was he saddened at having to give up the scepter of power? Apparently not. When asked what he did with the rare opportunity of being President for a day, Atchinson simply replied, "I went to bed."

President Zachary Taylor

No one can deny that President Zachary Taylor's life was filled with strange twists. He was late receiving word of his election to the Presidency in 1848, because the official notification came with postage due, and he refused to pay. As a matter of fact, he didn't even vote in that election. It wasn't until he was 62 years of age that he cast his first and last ballot.

The real irony in Taylor's life, however, focused on a controversy surrounding his death - a controversy which wasn't settled until just a few years ago.

On July 4, 1850, President Taylor was attending the groundbreaking ceremonies for the Washington monument. It just so happened that someone passed him a bowl of cherries and milk that warm afternoon, and he became ill. Five days later he was dead.

Immediately rumors began to spread that the President had been poisoned. Southerners distrusted him mightily over the slavery issue, and their criticism was so vitriolic that there were some who steadfastly maintained that "Old Rough and Ready" had been done in with a dose of arsenic.

They buried Taylor in Louisville, Kentucky, and as the years passed, the cloud of suspicion continued to linger. Finally in 1991, some historians convinced Taylor's descendants that indeed the President might have suffered arsenic poisoning. As a result, the President's remains were exhumed, and Kentucky's medical examiner brought samples of hair and fingernail tissue to Oak Ridge National Laboratory for study.

Working night and day, the scientists at the laboratory measured the level of arsenic in the hair and fingernail samples. They concluded that the amount of arsenic found was several hundred times less than they would have found if Taylor had died of arsenic poisoning. The President apparently had expired of natural causes.

So Zachary Taylor was returned to his plot in Louisville and laid to rest for a second time. He had served his country one final time by putting an end to rumors that he had been the victim of a well-planned conspiracy. In this case it was fiction that was stranger than truth.

Franklin Pierce

The Presidential campaign of 1852 was a rough and tumble affair, and when dark horse candidate, Franklin Pierce, captured the Democratic nomination, Mrs. Pierce was more than surprised. She was terrified. She had a strong premonition that something bad was going to happen, and it did, but it sure wasn't what she had imagined.

Two months later, in January, 1853, the train pulled away from the station in Andover, Massachusetts. It had only one passenger car, but it carried a very special traveler. Franklin Pierce, the President-elect of the United States was on his way to be sworn in as the nation's 14th Chief Executive. Mrs. Pierce and 11 year-old Benjamin sat beside him. She remained uneasy.

The train left the depot at 12:15 P.M. on that freezing

January afternoon. Pierce and his family settled in to watch the countryside slip by. They would not enjoy the view for very long.

President-elect Pierce was looking out the window. It was now 12:20 P.M. Suddenly he felt a severe shock. The front axle had broken, and the car was being dragged along the tracks. In another second, it was thrown over a rocky ledge and turned over twice before it hit the bottom.

After a few moments of moans and groans, it looked as if no one had been seriously hurt and that everybody was accounted for. Then Mrs. Pierce cried out that she couldn't find Benjamin. The President-elect rushed down the embankment to the splintered car that had broken in half. There he spied his son. The father gently picked up the lifeless body and carried it back to where Mrs. Pierce was sitting. Benjamin Pierce was no longer lost.

The Pierces buried their last child and went on to Washington. The President was forced to turn from the tragedy and deal with the monumental issues that faced the country. Mrs. Pierce, however, could find no such solace. She became a recluse, unable to carry out her duties as First Lady, and she never forgave herself.

All the time, her premonitions of tragedy had caused her to fear for her husband's life. She had been afraid that someone would assassinate him. She never dreamed that the needle of her extrasensory perception was pointing to little Benjamin, the last of her three children to be jerked from this life.

Mary Todd Lincoln

As Americans reflect upon their great Presidents, they almost invariably include Abraham Lincoln. Then just a surely as night follows day they begin to think about his wife, Mary. The President is always held to have been the more stable of the two, while Mary is often viewed as having been a basket case. Such a comparison, while possessing a modicum of truth, is patently one-sided. Mary may have had her emotional problems, but Honest Abe had his as well, especially when it came to "tying the knot."

Mary met Abe in Springfield, Illinois, where she lived with her sister. Their acquaintance blossomed into a friendship, and soon he was courting her. When he proposed, she accepted, never dreaming that he would be so difficult to get to the altar.

Abraham and Mary decided to have the shortest engagement in the history of Springfield. They would announce it at the beginning of the 1841 New Year's Day dinner and then actually exchange vows after desert.

With Mary's sister, Elizabeth, serving as hostess, all of the arrangements were made. On January 1, 1841, guests filled the house and champagne filled the glasses. By prearrangement, Lincoln was supposed to make his appearance precisely at 1:30 P.M. to announce his engagement to Mary Todd.

At the prescribed time, everyone stood holding their glasses and waiting. Five minutes passed and no Abraham. Ten minutes passed and still no Abraham. At 1:45, the assembled guests raised their glasses and toasted the New Year. At 2:00, Mary went upstairs and buried her face in her pillow while everyone else had dinner.

Abraham Lincoln never did show up that night, nor the next, nor the next. In fact, it was one year and eight months before she saw him again.

The reunion between Mary Todd and Abraham Lincoln was arranged in August of 1842, by mutual friends at Abraham's request. They stood in the parlor and eyed one another for a few moments, and then fell into each other's arms. Abraham could only explain that he was afraid. For her part, Mary didn't press him for an answer; she was just happy to have hold of him again. In a matter of minutes they were once more planning their wedding.

Mary and Abraham were finally married on Friday evening, November 4, 1842, and it was only when they were alone that night that Mary found out the real reason for Abraham's leaving her stranded on what was supposed to have been their wedding night almost two years before.

Mary Todd was not the first woman by that name whom Lincoln has asked to marry him. A few years before he had sought the hand of another Mary, although she was, according to Lincoln, fat, forty, toothless and weather beaten. To his amazement, this first Mary turned him down, and Lincoln developed such a complex that it almost cost him his second Mary, the one who through her own bizarre behavior, later made him realize just how sound of mind he really was.

The Lincoln Funeral Train

When President Lincoln was assassinated in 1865, Mary Lincoln decided to bury him in their hometown of Springfield, Illinois. His body was prepared, citizens of Washington DC. said their good-byes, and the funeral train pulled out of the station.

Lincoln's family was understandably grief-stricken, but oddly enough, only one of them made that long train trip with him back to Illinois. His wife, Mary Todd Lincoln was so overwrought, she couldn't be seen in public and needed young Tad Lincoln to remain with her. Robert Todd Lincoln was able to go only as far as Baltimore. That left just little Willie to accompany his father on that long journey home.

Willie had been born in Springfield in 1850. Of all of the Lincoln children, he was most like his father. He took an early interest in politics and religion and was a keen observer of everything around him.

In Illinois, he had been his father's constant companion, even when the elder Lincoln traveled to Chicago on business.

Where the father went, the son was sure to follow. That was as true as much in death as it was in life.

It took 13 days to bring Lincoln's body back to Springfield, and Willie rode with him every mile of the way. North to New York City - west to Chicago - south to Springfield, and at scores of stops in between, mourners paid homage to the fallen President, and Willie was right there.

When they took President Lincoln to Oak Ridge Cemetery in Springfield, Willie went right with him. He and his father would remain inseparable right to the end. Not even the tomb could keep them apart, for you see, young Willie Lincoln, like his father, had passed from this life as well.

In the winter of 1862, he had contracted typhoid fever and on February 20 of that year he died. Willie was buried in Georgetown, but when the President began his last trip home, they exhumed Willie and put him on the train with his father. The two caskets were carried across the country side by side, and when it came time for burial, they laid Willie to rest right beside his father. For 11 years they had been inseparable, and now not even the grave could divide them. Now they both belonged to the ages - together.

President Abraham Lincoln

Abraham Lincoln was a man full of apparent contradictions. He could be as serious as death one moment and telling funny stories the next. Today he might conduct himself as a statesman, and tomorrow he might exhibit the manners of a hillbilly. This incongruence extended right up to his last conscious moment, with the last words that he would ever hear.

The date was April 14, 1865. The place was Ford's Theatre in Washington D.C. For four long years, the President had labored under the stress of leading the nation in a bloody Civil War. Now it was all over. The Union had been preserved, and he could at last relax.

As the Lincolns took their seats in the Presidential box that Friday evening, their conversation centered around a desired trip to the Holy Land, which sentiment was entirely out of keeping with the play on stage, a story about an American backwoodsman who was visiting his refined English cousins.

Harry Hawk, the company stage manager who was doubling as the male comic lead, was raucously reciting the last words that the President would ever hear. On stage, a scheming mother had just discovered the American Cousin to be poor and mannerless.

"So I don't know the manners of good society, eh?' Hawk intoned." As he recited his lines, John Wilkes Booth, having gained entrance to the box, raised his pistol. "Well, I guess I know enough to turn you inside out, old gal," spouted Hawk on stage. Booth put the gun to the back of the President's head.

"You sockdolgizing old mantrap," mouthed Hawk, These were the last words that Abraham Lincoln ever heard. Booth pulled the trigger at that very instant.

Thus the man who so eloquently framed the nation's sentiment in his Gettysburg Address; the man whose intellect sparkled in the felicity of his language; the man who believed that words were more powerful than the sword, died with the words of a pun-filled comedy filling his ears.

President Abraham Lincoln

After a week of rain, the morning of April 14, 1865, was beautiful and bright. The war was over. It had lasted so long - this war between America and itself. More than 600,000 men had perished. Now no more boys would have to die - no more wasted blood.

On this the last morning of Abraham Lincoln's life, no one could miss noticing the difference about him. He just felt good again, all except for those dreams he kept having.

The President had planned an evening at Ford's Theatre for later that night. He had invited General and Mrs. Grant, but they declined. Curiously, thirteen other people proceeded to turn Lincoln down. In the end, however, Major Rathbone and his fiancee, Clara Harris, agreed to accompany Mr. and Mrs.

Lincoln.

At an 11:00 meeting of the cabinet that day, the President remarked that he had had two dreams that seemed so real. One related to water. Lincoln said he seemed to be in some vessel moving very fast. "I'm in a boat, and I drift and I drift. Gentlemen, something extraordinary is going to happen and very soon." The cabinet members twisted uncomfortably in their chairs, and then the President told them about the other dream he had a week earlier.

He had been stirred from his slumbers in a cold sweat. It had seemed so real and had been haunting him ever since. The President responded:

"I heard subdued sobs, as if a number of people were weeping. I left my bed and wandered downstairs.
I went from room to room until I arrived at theEast Room, which I entered. There before me was a corpse wrapped in funeral vestments. Around it were stationed soldiers who acted as guards.
'Who is dead in the White House?' I demanded of one of the soldiers. 'The President,' was his answer. 'He was killed by an assassin.'"

Every one knows the rest of the story. Lincoln was shot that night and died the next morning. It is all part of history. What we can't explain are his dreams. Did the President have a premonition of his death? That we will most likely never know, but Lincoln said at the time, "Most people nowadays regard dreams as foolish."

Still, it is interesting to ponder how history might have been changed if only the President had given his dreams a little more credence.

Lincoln's Funeral Procession

After Abraham Lincoln's assassination , a mortified nation felt obligated to do for him in death what it had been unable to do in life - that was to give him the full dignity that he deserved. They carried his remains to a tomb and declared that "Now he belonged to the ages." Unfortunately it would be another 36 years before his body would rest in peace.

On May 4, 1865, Abraham Lincoln's remains were placed in a limestone vault in Springfield's Oak Ridge Cemetery. In less than a year, they were removed to a temporary vault higher up the hill. Then in 1871, the almost completed Lincoln Tomb at the top of the hill received the body of the President, but he still was not to rest in peace.

In the autumn of 1876, a group of counterfeiters hatched a plan whereby they would break into the tomb, steal the body, and hold it for ransom. It almost worked. Lincoln's coffin was half out the door when lawmen swooped down and put an end to the caper.

Fearful of another attempt, Lincoln's friends now hid his coffin in a labyrinth of passageways beneath the obelisk at the top of the hill, and for the next ten years, the public paid homage to an empty sarcophagus. Finally in 1901, Robert Todd Lincoln decided that enough was enough.

He ordered a hole, thirteen feet deep, to be dug below the main catacomb floor. A four-foot base of cement was laid and an iron cage sunk into it. Then Lincoln's coffin was brought to the new burial site, but before he was lowered into his new resting place, an enterprising plumber cut a little window in the coffin, just above Lincoln's face - just to make sure it was really him. To the 17 people who peeked in, there was no question. The mole was there. He still had his beard - the nose, the chin - no doubt about it, it was Lincoln.

Today the body of Abraham Lincoln lies encased in tons of concrete, finally safe from all tampering or any other disturbance, short of a strong earthquake, and no longer susceptible to the prying eyes of the curious. Now he really does belong only to the Ages.

Lincoln's Replica Coffin

President Abraham Lincoln

The assassination of Abraham Lincoln by John Wilkes Booth has fascinated historians for years. Books, papers, and treatises on the tragedy abound, but a lot more could be written if scholars would take seriously the strange events that followed the death of our 16th President.

Consider Henry and Clara Rathbone, the young couple who attended Ford's Theatre with the Lincolns. They later moved to Germany, and he lost his mind, killed his wife, and ended up in an insane asylum.

Boston Corbett, the soldier who shot John Wilkes

Booth, went berserk during an 1887 meeting of the Kansas State Legislature. He was arrested and sent to the Topeka Asylum for the Insane.

William A Petersen, the German tailor in whose house the President died, committed suicide in 1871.

Ann Surratt, who tried to see President Andrew Johnson to plead for clemency for her mother, who was about to be executed for conspiring to kill the President, was prevented from doing so by two men: ex-Senator Preston King, and Senator James H. Lane.

On November 13, 1865, King tied a bag of bullets around his neck and committed suicide by jumping off a ferry boat on the Hudson River. The next year, on July 11, Lane shot himself to death in Fort Leavenworth, Kansas.

During the weeks following the assassination, Mary Todd Lincoln received a great deal of comfort in the White House from Dr. Anson G. Henry, who accompanied her back to Illinois. A few months later, on July 30, 1865, Dr. Henry drowned when the steamer in which he was a passenger, sank off the coast of California.

And as for Mary Todd Lincoln herself, a jury found her "... a fit person to be in a state hospital for the insane," and that's where she wound up in 1875.

Nearly everyone who was even remotely connected to the assassination of Lincoln suffered some devastating personal tragedy. If we didn't know better, we might think that a curse of some sort had been placed on those surrounding President Lincoln, including his own family.

Abraham and Tad Lincoln

Legacies are such interesting things. One solitary life often reverberates through the ages to influence generation upon generation. The descendants of John D. Rockefeller, Henry Ford, and Joseph Kennedy provide abundant examples. One that doesn't fit the mold, however, is Abraham Lincoln, and there's a very good reason for that.

At first blush, one would expect that being a direct descendant of Abraham Lincoln today would carry with it the aura and responsibility of Noblesse Oblige, but a close look at Lincoln's descendants reveals that nothing could be further from the truth.

Abraham Lincoln and Mary Todd Lincoln had four children, all boys: Robert, Edward, Willie, and Tad. Of these offspring, only Robert lived to maturity and provided the Lincolns with grandchildren. Edward died first, before Abraham was elected President. Willie went next in 1862, while the Lincolns were in the White House, and Tad lived just a few years after his father's tragic death. By 1871, just one of the offspring of Abraham Lincoln, Robert Todd Lincoln, survived.

Robert ultimately married, and he and his wife became the parents of three children, two daughters and a son. The boy, who was named Abraham after his grandfather, died at the age of 17, while his father was minister to Great Britain. That left the two daughters to vouchsafe the legacy of Abraham Lincoln.

In time each of the granddaughters of Abraham Lincoln married, one to a Mr. Isham and the other to a Mr. Beckwith. They each in turn gave birth to a single child, both boys. The Isham lad died early and without issue. At that point all hopes for keeping the Lincoln legacy in the family rested upon Robert Todd Lincoln Beckwith, the great-grandson of Abraham Lincoln.

Then in 1986, Beckwith died in his Washington D.C. home at the age of 86 and without heirs. Thus it was in that year, Abraham Lincoln's line came to an abrupt end. Today our 16th President has no direct descendants. Now only a grateful nation is left to carry his legacy. Come to think of it, that might not be so bad after all.

Robert Todd Lincoln

Robert Todd Lincoln lived a life filled with irony. As a young lad, he was rescued from a moving train by Edwin Booth, the elder brother of John Wilkes Booth, his father's assassin, but this was just the beginning of the strange twists of fate that Robert would encounter throughout his life.

Upon graduating from Harvard University, Lincoln joined the army and was assigned to General Ulysses S. Grant's staff. Later he served the United States as the last Minister to Great Britain, before the title was changed to Ambassador, and as United States Secretary of War under Garfield. He later became President of the Pullman Company of Chicago. Thus it was that on three occasions history was able to place Robert at the scene of a national tragedy.

He was in Washington D.C. on April 14, 1865, the night that his father was shot, and upon hearing the news rushed to his bedside where he maintained a vigil until the stricken President passed away. This, however, was not the last time that he would see a President die.

In 1881, Robert Todd Lincoln, as Secretary of War, was traveling with President James A. Garfield when he was shot in the Washington D.C. railroad station, and was with him when he later died.

Then in 1901, who do you think was invited to attend the Pan-American Exposition in Buffalo New York with President William McKinley? Robert Todd Lincoln! Thus he was on hand to witness the shooting of the 25th President of the United States and the third to be assassinated.

After the death of McKinley, Robert Todd Lincoln refused to attend any future presidential functions, and retired to his summer retreat in Manchester, Vermont, where he became a virtual recluse in his later years.

In 1926, Robert Todd Lincoln died, and they buried him in Vermont. Thus he became the only member of his father's immediate family not to be buried in the Lincoln family plot in Springfield, Illinois - one final twist to a life filled with strange coincidences.

Horace Greeley

Horace Greeley, the man who coined the phrase, "Go West, young man; go West," had a lot of irons in the fire. He founded the New York Tribune, devoted himself to the anti-slavery cause, and emersed himself in politics. In fact, he even ran for the U.S. Presidency in 1872, but lost, and it's a good thing for the country that he did.

Greeley had set himself on the path to national

prominence by the 1850s. He attended the first organizational meeting of the Republican party in 1856, and supported John C. Fremont, its first Presidential candidate.

Four years later he worked for the election of Abraham Lincoln, but abandoned him in 1864. Greeley supported the impeachment of President Andrew Johnson, and in 1868, campaigned for Ulysses S. Grant. Then the political porridge turned sour.

Grant got caught up in a number of financial scandals, and Greeley grew so disaffected with the Administration that he decided to run for the Presidency himself in 1872, on a "clean the house" platform.

From the start of the campaign, things didn't go well for Greeley. Because he had become the candidate of the Democratic Party, most of his former political cronies were now calling him a fool and a crank. Then on the eve of the election, his wife died. Finally, on election day the voters repudiated Horace Greeley by a huge margin. He was devastated and dreaded the vote of the Electoral College in December 1872.

Well, that was one indignity he would not have to suffer. On November 29, 1872, Greeley suffered a breakdown of mind and body and died. A few days later the electors met to conduct the REAL election of the President. Sixty-six of them cast their vote for Greeley and thus voted for a dead man!

So it was only through the vigilance of the Grim Reaper in 1872, that a constitutional crises was avoided. It appears the bard might have been right, at least in American politics, when he said, "There is a Divinity that shapes our ends, rough hew them as we will."

Rutherford B. Hayes   Samuel J. Tilden

The election was a dead heat. The popular vote was close, and neither candidate seemed to have a majority in the electoral college. Then all eyes turned toward Florida. Does this scenario sound familiar? Actually it describes the election of 1876, when shenanigans in Florida threw the nation into a tizzy.

In that year, Republican Rutherford B. Hayes and Democrat Samuel J. Tilden were running for President. When the vote was counted in November, no one had a majority in the Electoral College. The election hinged on the 19 electoral votes in Louisiana, South Carolina, and Florida, and the results in those three states were in dispute.

Charges and counter-charges flew, and things got so ugly that Congress had to create a special commission to decide the election. Five members of the panel came from the Senate - 3 Republicans and 2 Democrats. Five came from the House - 3 Democrats and 2 Republicans, and five came from the United States Supreme Court - two Democrats, two Republicans and one "independent" judge.

A close examination of the vote in South Carolina

and Louisiana put those states in Hayes' column. Then the Commission turned to Florida. Election officials there contacted the Tilden people and offered to make it impossible for the Commission to do anything other than award the state's electoral votes to him, and the price for such an assurance? $200,000 dollars.

"That seems to be the standard figure," Tilden remarked to a friend before he rejected the offer. The Democratic candidate was sure he wouldn't need it. He was certain that under the scrutiny of the Federal Election Commission, he would be awarded Florida's electors.

Much to Tilden's surprise, however, the Commission gave Florida - and the election - to Rutherford B. Hayes, who became the nation's 18th President. Tilden had prevailed in the popular vote by a margin of 247,000 votes, but in the Electoral College the tally stood at 185 to 184 in favor of Hayes and all because Tilden refused a bribe. One has to wonder how much things have changed in the Sunshine State over the past century or so?

President James A. Garfield

Life looked promising for James A. Garfield in 1880. He had just been elected President of the United States after a distinguished political and military career. As fate would have it, however, his life was cut short, due in no small measure to the bed on which he was placed after he was shot by an assassin.

James Garfield was elected as the 20th President of the United States. He had been a Civil War general and a long tenured member of the House of Representatives. When he took the oath of office in March of 1881, nobody expected that just a few months later, a mournful nation would bury its second assassinated President.

On July 2, 1881, in a Washington railroad station, Charles Giteau, an embittered attorney, who had sought a consular post, shot the President. They carried the wounded Chief Executive to the White House, and there he lingered for two months.

Physicians from all over the country were called in to help save the President's life. Through all of July and August, Garfield's doctors kept their vigil, attempting to solve one very perplexing problem. The medics couldn't find the bullet in Garfield's body. They felt and probed for days on end with no luck. Finally, somebody suggested sending for Alexander Graham Bell, inventor of the telephone. Perhaps his latest invention, the metal detector, would do the job.

Alas, not even the likes of the man who invented the telephone could find that bullet. Bell's induction-balance electrical device went inexplicably haywire every time it was passed over the President's body.

On September 19, 1881, the hidden bullet did its work, and the President died from the infection it caused. It was only after his funeral, that Bell solved the mystery of the failure of his invention to find the bullet. Garfield had been placed on a bed with metal springs, and no one thought to move him.

Thus it was that in an effort to make the President comfortable, his attendants sealed his fate. Who knows? One of those old-fashioned feather beds might have changed the course of American history.

President Benjamin Harrison

Every school child knows that California was our country's 31st state, and kids in Delaware know their state was the first. Indeed an important part of the history of every state includes the order in which it entered the Union. That's why teachers scratch their heads when they come to that part of the history of North and South Dakota.

In the beginning, there was no North Dakota nor South Dakota - only Dakota Territory. Then in 1883, they moved the capital from Yankton to Bismarck, and the squabble began. The folks in the southern part of the territory felt cheated, so they applied for statehood, but Congress. turned them down.

The discontent created by the capital shift in 1883, sparked a second, more sophisticated attempt, to create the state of South Dakota out of the southern half of the territory. Voters approved a state constitution and a full slate of officers.

The legislature and state officials organized the new state government. Senators were chosen, but once again, Washington refused to grant statehood.

Finally, in 1889, the growing political pressure forced the federal government to act. The Dakota Territory was split in two, and preparations were made to admit the 39th and 40th states of the Union. There was, however, one more thorn in the side of the body politic that would require the wisdom of Solomon. Which one of the new states, North or South Dakota, would be admitted first? Which one would become the 39th state of the Union, and which one the 40th? While the local politicians fought over the dilemma, President Benjamin Harrison came up with the solution.

At the signing of the proclamation admitting the two new states, the President put each document inside identical newspapers. He then shuffled them back and forth until no one could tell which paper held which state's admission papers. Just enough of the statehood documents were left exposed for the President to sign. Harrison put his signature to both documents, and after one final shuffle, they were removed. North Dakota and South Dakota were now states, but because of the President's ingenious shell game, no one will ever know which of the documents was signed first, and folks in the Dakotas will never know whether their state was actually the 39th or 40th to join the Union.

Former President Theodore Roosevelt Giving a Speech

Although short in stature, Teddy Roosevelt was really a giant of a man. Nothing could stop him when he made up his mind to do something. Take that day in 1912, for instance. Not even a bullet could keep him from finishing a job he had set out to do.

The date was October 12. There was a three way race for the White House, and former President Theodore Roosevelt was on the stump for the Progressives, or the Bull Moose party, as it was popularly known.

Running on the Democratic ticket was the Princeton professor, Woodrow Wilson, and for the Republicans, the incumbent, William Howard Taft.

The Progressives had moved very quickly to kick off the campaign by putting Roosevelt out on the trail. That's why he was in Milwaukee on that fateful day. On his way to the auditorium, where he was to speak, the former President was shot in the chest by an unknown gunman at close range.

Fortunately for Roosevelt the bullet first went through the thick manuscript he was preparing to speak from, before it struck his metal eyeglass case. The two obstructions reduced the velocity of the bullet before it entered his body.

Doctor's examined T.R. and ordered him to the hospital at once, but he steadfastly refused to be denied his opportunity to speak to the crowd, and proceeded to the rostrum to give the speech with the bullet still in his chest. He began the oration with the following words: "Friends, I shall ask you to be as quiet as possible. I don't know whether you fully understand that I have just been shot, but it takes more than that to kill a Bull Moose."

Well, Roosevelt didn't win the election. Despite this speech, he finished second. Nevertheless, he sure made history. Today it is hard to imagine the kind of tenacity that would keep a candidate pressing flesh with a bullet in his chest.

TWISTS

FROM THE

WEST

Dr. Marcus Whitman

Dr. Marcus Whitman was a New York physician who dedicated his life to missionary work among the Cayuse Indians of old Oregon. He and his wife, Narcissa, lived among the tribe for eleven years, until that measles epidemic hit. When the Doctor couldn't cure the illness, it cost him his life, but it wasn't because he contacted the disease.

Once they were in old Oregon, which included the present day states of Oregon, Washington, and Idaho, the Whitmans built a lean-to mission among the Cayuse Indians near Fort Walla Walla, and attempted, alternating between success and failure, to persuade them to depart from their own culture and adopt a new religion and a new way of life. Then came the crisis of 1847. By then, pioneers were moving into the Northwest by the hundreds, bringing with them diseases previously unknown to the area. One of these maladies was measles, and it promptly decimated large numbers of the Cayuse tribe.

Not surprisingly, the Cayuse correctly made the connection between the presence of the devastating measles epidemic and the influx of Anglo pioneers. They blamed the Whitmans for the hordes of Whites who were invading their lands. By November 29, 1847, 197 Cayuse lives had been taken by measles or dysentery, so the Indians held a council and decided to make their move.

That night Chief Tiloukaikt rapped at the Whitman's door, explaining that he was in need of medicine. The Doctor let the Chief in, as well as a sub-chief, Thomas. While Thomas held Whitman's attention, Tiloukaikt dispatched him with a tomahawk. Then the other doors were opened and the rest of the execution party entered to complete their desired intent.

Before the night was over, ten Whites were killed including Marcus and Narcissa. Their bodies lay where they fell for days until soldiers came and buried them. In 1897, the remains of the Whitmans were disinterred and reburied in a common grave with appropriate ceremonies, and over the new burial site was placed a marble slab dedicated to the memory of the couple who couldn't cure the measles and paid for it with their lives.

Narcissa

Generalissimo Antonio Lopez de Santa Anna

No one can say that folks from Texas don't take their history seriously. Back in 1986, when the Lone Star State was celebrating the Sesquicentennial of the Republic of Texas, officials there tried to retrieve the Mexican flag that had flown over the Alamo in 1836. Needless to say, they didn't have any luck - not even when they tried to trade Santa Anna's leg for it.

As most everyone knows, on March 6, 1836, the Alamo fell to the forces of General Santa Anna. Two years later in a comic opera war with the French at Veracruz, Mexico, known as the "French Pastry War," Santa Anna lost his left leg to a cannonball. The Napoleon of the West was fitted with an artificial leg made of cork.

Then in 1847, during the war with the United States, a contingent of troops from Illinois swooped through and Santa Anna fled, leaving behind his cork leg. Eventually it wound up in the Illinois State Military Museum in Springfield, and that's where it lay practically unnoticed until those folks in Texas asked the Mexican government for the return of the flag that flew over the Alamo.

Mexico took the request under advisement and decided to cooperate IF the Texans would reciprocate. Our neighbors south of the border wanted to have Santa Anna's leg back. In return, they would send the Alamo's flag.

Immediately hopes in Texas soared. and then came crashing down. In spite of all the politicians in Austin could do, nothing could persuade the curator of the Illinois museum to part with the leg.

"We have no intention of giving it up," said Colonel O. Johnson. "There have been several attempts by the Mexican Government to obtain the leg - the last in 1942 - but it's still ours." And that was the final word on the matter.

Texas had to celebrate the 150th birthday of the Republic without that famous banner, and the left leg of Generalissimo Antonio Lopez de Santa Anna - the cork one - never made it back to Mexico. Apparently some actions of the past are just not capable of correction.

Sam Houston

History has always viewed Sam Houston as a rough and ready frontiersman. He's remembered for his exploits as an adopted warrior of the Cherokee Nation, the liberator of Texas from the oppressive sword of Santa Anna, and the first President of the Lone Star Republic. Throughout his tumultuous career, no one ever thought that Houston would ever have a soft spot in his heart for religion. Little did they know!

In 1850, the Reverend George Washington Baines was installed as pastor of the Independence Baptist Church. Now it just so happened that this cleric, who would one day become the great-grandfather of President Lyndon Baines Johnson, had as one of his parishioners, Mrs. Sam Houston, a most devout woman. At the urging of Mrs. Houston, the Reverend Baines had a number of lengthy discussions with the General concerning his spiritual welfare. At the conclusion of one of these sessions, Houston agreed to be baptized and join the church.

When word got out that Sam Houston had found religion, more than a few were skeptical, and a handful were downright irreverent. On November 19, 1854, the day set aside for the baptism, pranksters filled the makeshift baptistery at Kounty Creek with limbs and other debris. Undaunted, the baptizing party moved to Little Rocky Creek. There Houston made his public statement and ascended from the waters spluttering, "Reverend, you've baptized my pocket book." "Thank God," replied the preacher, "I wish it could have happened to the pocketbook of every Baptist."

According to a church periodical, the announcement of General Houston's immersion excited the wonder and surprise of many who had supposed that he was "past praying for." The editor of the bulletin went on to state, however, that Houston's conversion was no marvel to him, for over 3,000 clergymen had been praying for the General because of some of his antics in the United States Senate.

And what was Sam Houston's attitude toward this public reaction to his conversion? It's best summed up in a remark he made to a friend, who upon hearing the news, commented, "Well, General, I hear your sins were washed away the other day." Houston calmly answered with a wry smile, "Yes, that's true. Lord help the fish."

Monterey in 1842

The United States officially acquired California from Mexico in February of 1848, but it had had its eye on the province for a long time. In fact six years earlier, the American Navy captured the capital, Monterey, much to everyone's chagrin. The entire fiasco turned out to be a comedy of errors - it's just that not very many people were laughing.

In the fall of 1842, the Pacific Ocean was full of warships. Everybody was casting a hungry eye at the weakly held provincial capital of Monterey, and leading the pack was Commodore Thomas Jones of the USS United States. He was under orders that California was not to fall into the hands of any power other than the United States. The problem was that he had to be careful and not start a war with precipitate action. The Commodore couldn't allow the French or the English to beat him to the punch, but neither could he move against Mexico without a good reason. That justification came to him on October 19, 1842.

A rumor reached his flag ship that Mexico and the United States were at war over Texas. "Strike - Strike now," came the advice from his officers, so he struck. At 9:00 the next morning, he sent 150 marines ashore, and they hauled down the Mexican flag and ran up the Stars and Stripes. California now belonged to the United States.

There was, however, a problem. The rumor had no truth. The United States was NOT at war with Mexico, so the Commodore in effect said "Ooops, Sorry," to the Californios, and hurriedly replaced the American standard with the Mexican flag.

Thus, in October of 1842, the United States had possession of California for about 30 hours, until Jones learned of his mistake. The Mexican government was of course angry, and it wasn't until January of 1843 that they formally forgave the Americans - for a price. They demanded 10,000 dollars, 80 military uniforms, and a set of instruments from the band on Jones' ship. So in a sense, the short-lived capture of Mexican California by the United States in 1842 was something of a musical comedy.

John C. Fremont

John C. Fremont is a legend in American history, in part because he played such an important role in the drama of conquest in which California was transformed from a province of Mexico into a state of the Union. It seems a shame that the people so quickly forgot.

Fremont led the California Battalion in the war with Mexico and in January of 1847, General Andres Pico surrendered his forces to the great pathfinder. After a short stretch as military governor, however, Fremont got caught in a power struggle between the army and the navy. As a result he was taken back east and court-martialed.

Nevertheless, by 1849, Fremont was back in California mining his rich quartz vein on his Mariposa ranch. Before the year was out, he had been elected, along with William M. Gwin, to represent the new state in the United States Senate, so back to Washington he went. And that's when he got into trouble again.

Before Fremont and Gwin could be seated, they had to draw straws to decide who would get the long term of six years and who would get the short term of just one session. John lost and was destined to serve just 21 days as Senator from California.

At that time, the debate over slavery was raging, and California's two newly elected senators were on opposite sides. Gwin was a former slave owner and proponent of the peculiar institution. Fremont, on the other hand, was adamant in his opposition to human bondage.

Back home, in California, however, the pro-slavery forces were powerful - so powerful that when the 1850 session of Congress was over, they were able to dump John C. Fremont. He made it easy for them. He didn't campaign at all. Rather, he isolated himself on his mining claim in Mariposa and was defeated.

So John C. Fremont, explorer, soldier, and senator, soon found out what every great leader has come to know. The public was fickle, and fame was fleeting, especially in those early days of California statehood.

John C. Freemont

"Dr. Joe Meek"

When Americans began drifting into California in the 1840's, most of them thought that they were coming to one of the healthiest climates in the world. As a matter of fact, though, people got just as sick here as they did any place else. That's why some of the first pioneers became doctors. The only problem was none of them had any credentials.

Dr. John Marsh was the first California pioneer to become a doctor without benefit of the Hippocratic oath. He used his Harvard diploma, written in Latin, which few Californios could read, to prove that he was qualified to take care of the sick. So qualified was he, that Marsh charged 25 cow hides, the common currency of the day, for a home visit.

Marsh, the heroic fraud, was then followed by two more makeshift practitioners, Joe Meek and G.M. Waseurtz. Meek could neither read nor write, but that didn't stop him. When the colorful mountain man came down from Oregon to Monterey, he cheerfully announced that he was a physician. One of his very first patients was a young Mexican lad who had cut off his toe with an ax. Meek stuck the boy's toe back on with mud, and it grew. From then on, nobody around Monterey had any trouble referring to Meek as Doctor.

The third man to enter the medical field was Waseurtz. He too wound up in Monterey, and because of his knowledge of botany and minerals, the Natives concluded that he was a "Medico."

Waseurtz replied that since he could look grave and was looking for a business opportunity, he suddenly became a doctor. "I laid down some broad principles," wrote Waseurtz. "One was to charge well, and the other was never to prescribe anything that was not disagreeable to take."

Thus as California prepared to receive the thousands of pioneers during the gold rush, the California Medical Society consisted of Doctor John Marsh, Doctor Joe Meek, and Doctor G.M. Waseurtz, all of them charging high prices and apparently only mildly impeding the curative abilities of Mother Nature.

Sutter's Mill in 1848

California became a part of the United States at the conclusion of the war between the United States and Mexico. On February 2, 1848, officials of the two nations signed the Treaty of Guadalupe Hidalgo, and Mexico relinquished title to California, in exchange for 15 million dollars.

Just nine days earlier, however, a self-employed utility man named James Marshall made a discovery that he tried to keep secret. One has to wonder if the Mexican officials wouldn't have held out for a better deal if only the cat had been let out of the bag a bit sooner?

Marshall was working for Captain John Sutter in 1847, when he was dispatched to build a sawmill on the North Fork of the American River. On January 24, 1848, he found two gold nuggets in the millrace. Excitedly he swore his workers to secrecy while he rode back to Sutter's Fort to consult with the Captain.

When it was determined that the find was actually gold, Sutter also urged secrecy. He didn't want anything to upset the agricultural empire that he had spent 10 years building. Sutter reckoned, however, without the industrious Sam Brannan.

Somehow the merchant/newspaperman found out about Marshall's discovery. Knowing that an influx of gold seekers would benefit his merchantile efforts, he saddled his horse and headed for San Francisco with dust and nuggets in hand and shouting the news of the discovery. Almost overnight, San Francisco was deserted. The rush for gold had begun.

Before the year was out, California had yielded over ten million dollars worth of gold, 2/3 the price that the United States had to pay for most of the southwest.

So Mexico gave up California for a pittance, and the United States became the beneficiary. One can only wonder how the Treaty of Guadalupe Hidalgo would have been altered if the timing of history had not been on the side of the Americans.

First gold found by James Marshall

James Marshall

California was in great turmoil in 1844. The people had risen up against Micheltoreno, their Governor sent from Mexico City. It was an ill-fated exercise with one very significant result. It denied Pablo Gutierrez the honor of walking onto the pages of history and opened the way for James Marshall to take credit for being the one who first discovered gold in California.

There had never been any love lost between the Californios, as the Mexican natives of California were called, and the governors who were sent north from Mexico City to run the province. By 1844, an armed revolt broke out.

Now it just so happened that in the autumn of that year, Pablo Gutierrez who worked for Captain John Sutter, came into the Fort with some astounding news. He claimed to have discovered gold somewhere in the Sierra Nevada Mountains. Gutierrez secretly confided in another Sutter employee, John Bidwell, and prepared to show him where he made his find.

Before the pair could leave the fort, however, Sutter received word of the outbreak of hostilities on the coast, so he dispatched Gutierrez to carry word to Governor Micheltoreno that he could count on Sutter. Unfortunately for Pablo, the Captain committed his fealty in writing, and as Gutierrez reached Gilroy, he was captured by the rebel forces. When Sutter's letter to Governor Micheltorena was discovered, Pablo was strung up to the nearest tree.

All the while, John Bidwell waited at Sutter's Fort, unaware of Gutierrez' demise. He had his pick and shovel all packed and was ready to go, until a courier brought the news that Pablo Gutierrez was dead, as was Bidwell's dream of striking it rich. He didn't know where Pablo had found the gold.

Insofar as Governor Micheltoreno packed up and went home, the insurrection was successful. Bidwell, in the meantime, went back to work for John Sutter and forgot about gold until that new carpenter, James Marshall, made his lucky find on the south fork of the American River in 1848.

History well remembers James Marshall for his discovery, but in actuality, had it not been for the political turmoil that preceded that find, today we might be reading how Pablo Gutierrez found the first nugget of California gold.

Captain John Sutter

On January 24, 1848, gold was discovered at John Sutter's sawmill on the American River. For a few weeks it remained a secret, but then the word leaked out, and the world rushed in. One would have thought that this would have made Captain Sutter happy. As things turned out, the discovery sent him back to the poor house.

It was money troubles that had driven John Sutter from his native Switzerland in the first place. To escape a debtor's prison, he immigrated to California in 1839. There he was given almost 50,000 acres by the Mexican Governor. Sutter built it into an empire and called it New Helvetia.

Sutter's trapping, agriculture, and cattle raising enterprise prospered beyond belief. In addition, Sutter's Fort became the focal point for the increasing flow of covered wagons bringing settlers from the United States. Everything was coming up roses until he decided to send James Marshall to build that sawmill at Coloma over 150 years ago.

When Marshall discovered gold in the millrace of the sawmill, it was all over for Sutter. The secret soon leaked out, and his own workers abandoned him for the gold fields. Squatters and miners overran his lands, dispersed and slaughtered his cattle, and destroyed his fields. By 1852, New Helvetia was in complete disarray.

Sutter, now hopelessly in debt once more, traveled to Washington D.C. He spent his remaining years pleading with the federal government to compensate him for his loss, but it was all to no avail. His claims were denied, and he died in the poverty that he had tried so hard to escape.

For almost 10 years, Captain John Sutter had been the acknowledged major-domo of the Sacramento Valley, and it must have been truly a bitter pill to swallow when he had the rug jerked out from under him by the discovery of gold.

In retrospect, it is not surprising that he wanted to keep the find a secret - not because he wanted to keep all that gold to himself - no, what he really wanted was a wilderness over which he could rule, and for awhile he had it, until James Marshall came out of the hills with those two little pieces of gold.

Levi Strauss

In the early part of 1850, a young man stepped off the gangplank in San Francisco harbor. He was bound for the gold regions of Northern California. His intentions were to head for Hangtown and there to pan for gold. Instead, he struck it rich with a pair of pants, and as a result, his name became a household word.

In the young man's luggage, all that his ticket would allow, were items not usually selected for a gold mining venture. Before leaving New York he had, with the help of his two brothers, gathered a small stock of merchandise composed of heavy canvas and rough materials. This was to be his grubstake. He had figured, rightly so, that goods of this character might bring a fancy price in the West and that he might be able to sell them and obtain enough cash to go into gold mining in a big way.

The man had hardly been ashore a few hours before a passing miner hailed him on the street, asking him what he had in his bundles. Upon hearing his explanation, the miner disgustedly shook his head and said what he should have brought along were men's pants, complaining that the only ones available in the gold fields would not hold up under the hard labors at the mines.

Now the young traveler was not one to pass up an opportunity. He straightway piloted his new friend and first customer to the nearest tailor and told him to make up a pair of pants for each of them from his stock of canvas. The miner was elated with the tough fabric and proudly displayed them among his friends in San Francisco. As the months passed the young man was so busy furnishing material for miner's pants, that his gold mining venture had to be postponed. Everyone wanted a pair of the pants which the tailors were making from his canvas.

And that's how "Levi's" became a tradition in the Old West. Just as western hats invariably became known as "Stetsons" and revolvers as "Colts," so were cowboy pants described by westerners and writers as Levi's, and all because Levi Strauss came to California and mined the miners instead of the mines.

Mr. and Mrs. James F. Reed

James F. Reed was a very prosperous Illinois merchant. He lived not far from Abraham and Mary Lincoln on 8th Street in Springfield. In 1846, Reed decided to join the Donner party in their tragic trek west, but before they got to California, Reed was banished from the group and was left in the desert to die. As things turned out, however, that punishment wound up saving his life.

After reaching Fort Bridger, the ill-fated Donner Party made the mistake of taking the Hastings Cut-off and lost 30 to 40 days in so doing. Nerves became frayed and tempers ran short. Two of Reed's companions, John Snyder and Milt Elliot began to quarrel, and when Reed intervened, Synder beat him with a bull whip. James defended himself with a knife and sank it deep into Snyder's chest.

On October 5, 1846, the party held a meeting and decreed that although his family could remain, James Frazier Reed would have to go. He was banished without a gun or food into the wilderness. Meanwhile, the rest of the Donner Party plodded on toward their rendezvous with destiny.

By November 1, 1846, the group was just three miles from the summit of the Sierra Nevada when the first hard snows hit. They were trapped. Several aborted attempts were made to breach the pass, but they failed. As everyone knows the Donner Party then had to resort to cannibalism.

Then in February of 1847, who should appear in their camp but James F. Reed. He had made it to Sutter's Fort all by himself and now led a rescue party back to his family and stranded comrades - the very ones who had consigned him to death in the desert just a few months prior.

In the end, 45 members of the Donner Party survived while 34 perished, and among those who made it were the Reeds. While their father's expulsion had all the trappings of a tragedy at the time, it was in reality a blessing in disguise. Who knows what would have happened to the family if they had been forced to stay up in those mountains where human flesh was all that kept some people alive.

Jefferson Hunt

It was October of 1849, and time was running out for the Jefferson Hunt Wagon Train. They had heard stories of the Donner Party and decided to avoid that fate by heading south from Utah Lake along the eastern side of the Sierra Nevada, into Los Angeles, and then up to the gold fields. As things turned out, they would have been much better off to take their chances against the snow.

It was October 9 when the party headed south, and they would have been all right if only Captain Smith had not convinced most of them to take a short cut through Walker Pass and into the Tulare Valley. Short cuts always sounded good on the trail, so they took it, never knowing what they were about to endure.

In a few days they were facing the wind-blown wastes of a sun-baked desert with mountains all around. They had no choice but to press on.

They abandoned most of their wagons, and packed their belongings on their failing oxen. But without water, their tongues soon were swollen; their lips cracked. The oxen laid down in the sand, never to rise again.

The first to die of thirst was the Rev. Mr. Fish. The next to go was William Isham, who crawled four miles on his hands and knees in search of water. In camp, the men with burnt faces and skeletal frames lay down and waited for death.

By January of 1850, they were emaciated from dysentery and exhaustion. One poor fellow said, "I will just take a little nap" and never woke up.

When the party finally reached the top of the range on the western side of the dreary wasteland, they turned around and surveyed what they had just crossed. They appropriately named it Death Valley, for that was what it was and still is.

What started out as an attempt to avoid the fate of the Donner Party, turned out to be a nightmare of about the same proportions. The only difference was they didn't eat each other.

Death Valley, California

Pioneers traveled West in long wagon trains

There were 69 wagons in Edwin Bryant's train, and 67 of them carried women and children. As one of the officers of the company, Bryant was more than a little worried about the safety of the younger travelers. Actually, he was afraid of hostile Indians, but there was a more real danger. Those rolling wagon wheels were as dangerous as any Indian arrow.

After Bryant and his group left Independence, Missouri, they traveled northwest, crossing the Big Blue and Kansas Rivers. When they reached the Platte River they headed due west, and that's when tragedy struck. A young lad of about 8 years fell from the side of a loaded wagon, and one of the rear wheels ran over his leg, crushing it to pieces. There being no doctor with the party, Bryant did his best to apply first aid. He bandaged it and put the child in the back of his mother's wagon.

After five or six days, the boy began to scream that he could feel something moving on his injured leg. Upon removing the bandages, the wounds were found to be covered with maggots. There was nothing else to do but amputate. With a wood saw as the only instrument, no one would volunteer to perform the operation, the pleas from the mother notwithstanding. Finally, Bryant stepped forward and grabbed the saw. His gruesome task was hardly half completed when the child fell back in shock and soon died.

They buried the boy beside the trail and ran the wagons back and forth over his grave to keep it safe from predators, and then they went on. Later they would face those Indian arrows that Bryant feared so much, and some of them found their mark. None however scarred the memory of Edwin Bryant as much as the little lad who fell victim to the inexorable roll of wagon wheels moving west.

A woman during the Californian gold rush

During the California gold rush, the very sight of a woman would often be enough to set an entire mining camp into a frenzy. More often than not, it worked to the distinct advantage of the woman, like that time in the foothills above Sacramento when gender distinctions definitely paid off.

It was just about daybreak when the first miner arose and discovered that some newcomers had arrived during the night. He moseyed down to their wagon, and to his surprise and delight, there was a calico dress hanging on one of the wagon wheels.

The over-joyed miner ran from tent to tent waking up the entire camp and informing them that there was a woman in their midst. Soon every tent was emptied of its inhabitants as a bevy of grizzled miners, shook the sleep out of their eyes to see for themselves.

Sure enough not 100 yards away, there was the prairie schooner with the dress fluttering in the wind, giving it the look of the flagship of femininity. A shout of delight and expectation went up from the crowd of miners and suddenly a man's face appeared through the burlap cover of the wagon.

The miners cried in unison, "Fetch her out."
"It is my wife," replied the newcomer. "She is sick, we have been robbed of money, provisions, and everything by the Indians. We want to rest."
"Fetch her out!" insisted the miners. We've got to see her."
"But gentlemen, the poor thing, she..."
"Fetch her out" demanded the miners.

So with some trepidation, he did as he was told. When the woman appeared, they sent up three rousing cheers, crowded around and stared at her in disbelief. They listened to her voice and touched her dress and then they collected twenty-five hundred dollars in gold and gave it to the shocked husband.

Then in twos and threes they wandered back to their own camps, content that they had once more been in the presence of a woman. As for the man and his wife, they departed the next night. After all, there might be other mining camps whose inhabitants were just as desperate for a look at a member of the opposite sex.

Charlie Parkhurst was a stagecoach driver for Wells Fargo & Company

Charlie Parkhurst was a stagecoach driver in the Old West. Everybody had heard of him, for he was one of the most skilled teamsters around. That's why folks were so shocked when they discovered Charlie's secret in 1868.

Charlie Parkhurst, or One-eyed Charlie, or Cockeyed Charlie, as he was variously known, because he had lost an eye when kicked by a horse, quickly became a legend.

He began to earn his reputation when he encountered holdup men along his route. The first time, he threw down his strong box without a single demurrer. The second time, however, it was a different story. He was prepared. As the would-be bandit stepped out into the middle of the road, Charlie aimed a shotgun blast into the chest of the outlaw, whipped his horses into a full gallop, and left the highwayman in the middle of the road.

After that, One-eyed Charlie became known as one

of the toughest, roughest, and most daring of the stagecoach drivers in California.

One time while navigating his team around a particularly dusty curve, a passenger asked, "How in the world can you see your way through this dust?"

"I can smell the way," answered Charlie. "Fact is, I've traveled over these mountain roads so often, I can tell where the road is by the sound of the wheels. When they rattle, I'm on hard ground; when they don't rattle, I generally look over the side to see where she's a going."

Charlie continued to whip up a team until his death in 1868, and that's when folks got the surprise of their lives. One can only imagine the shock that reverberated across the countryside when the undertaker informed the people that Charlie wasn't really a man after all.

That rugged stage driver - the one outlaws avoided and fellow drivers saluted was really a woman. All this time he/she had fooled the people with a good disguise, and proved that anything a man could do, she could do better.

John C. Fremont

The name of John C. Fremont will forever be linked to the Westward Movement and the conquest of California. The great pathfinder came to the Golden State in 1846, determined to make a name for himself in the upcoming war with Mexico. In the end, he did just that, but not before the Californios made him the laughing stock of the countryside.

Captain Fremont and his party of 60 armed riflemen

showed up near Monterey in early 1846. He claimed that he was simply there to make maps of the area and assured the Mexican authorities that he would soon leave, and probably would have done so if he had not been challenged by Manuel Castro. The Mexican Commandante ordered Fremont to leave forthwith, and Fremont took umbrage at the ultimatum.

Leading his men to the top of Hawk's Peak in the Gavilan Mountains overlooking San Juan Bautista, he hastily built a little log fort, ran up the American flag, and waited on the enemy. They weren't long in coming.

On March 5, Fremont could see the Mexican army assembling at the foot of the hill. The Captain gave out the orders: "If we are attacked, we will fight to the extremity and refuse quarter. If we are hemmed in, we will die, all of us, under the flag of our country." At face value, it looked as if Fremont was toeing the mark, but when the Mexicans began to advance up the hill, the Captain went to plan B.

After a slight wind came along and blew down the American flag, Fremont took it as an omen and led his men down the escape hatch that existed on the back side of the mountain.

Fremont didn't stop running until he reached the Oregon border, where he learned that a state of war existed between the United States and Mexico. With this knowledge he wheeled around and marched back to Sutter's Fort to assume his legendary role in the conquest of California and to live down the embarassment of having turned tail and having run in his first encounter with the Californios.

The Phrenologist defends his reading

The mid-nineteenth century was a great age for medical quacks, and California certainly had its share during the gold rush. Among the most notorious were the phrenologists who claimed to be able to tell the character of a man by feeling the bumps on his head. Most of the time the public was fairly tolerant, until one pseudo-scientist got a bit too personal in 1850.

When one poor Kentucky farmer went broke in the California gold fields, he turned to practicing phrenology to put some meat with the beans. Every Sunday he would gather the miners around him to feel their heads and postulate on their moral make-up.

At one of these sessions, the crowd was especially large and appeared quite interested. Everybody wanted his cranium examined, including John David Borthwick. When it came his turn, John took off his hat and gave the phrenologist permission to feel his head.

The man gave him a very elaborate synopsis of his character, and if he had left it at that, he would have been home free. At that moment, however, the phrenologist spotted a most interesting specimen, one he couldn't pass up.

He invited the subject to the front, and according to John Borthwick made a fateful miscalculation. Fingering the man's head with vigor, the phrenologist ascribed to his subject a most dreadful character. He called him a liar, a cheat, and a thief. He even went so far as to assert that the man would murder his own father for an ounce of gold if given the chance.

Well, that was a risky assessment, especially in the wild and woolly West. In the twinkling of an eye, the Phrenologist had some peculiar bumps of his own. The indignant miner bloodied the man's nose and blackened his eyes. In short, he got the whipping of his life.

After the would-be scientist received his thrashing, he left California for his old Kentucky home. He might not have made much money there, but at least he could paw his neighbors' head to his heart's content without any fear of retribution.

Pioneer wagon train

One of the strangest tales in American history is recorded in the diary of Elizabeth Geer. She and her husband and their seven children set out in a covered wagon from Indiana headed for California in 1847. The wagon train with which the Geers were traveling reached the half way point by September 15. On the morning of the 16th, one of the men reported that he was having trouble.

His wife was angry at him for trying to drag her half way across the continent and refused to take another step west. Not only would she not budge, she wouldn't allow her children to go either. Her husband had had his oxen hitched up to the wagons for three hours and had been coaxing her to hop aboard, but she wouldn't stir.

Elizabeth told her husband what was taking place, and he gathered three male companions and went to consult with the recalcitrant woman. When she steadfastly refused their entreaties to join them, they grabbed her young ones and crammed them in the wagon. Her husband then drove off and left her sitting.

As the wagons rolled west, the abandoned woman got up, took the back track and traveled out of sight. Meanwhile, the husband sent his oldest son back to where they had camped to retrieve a horse that he had left. In less than an hour, having cut across a bend in the road, the wife overtook her husband. When he saw her he asked, "Did you meet Son John?"

"Yes" was the reply, "and I picked up a stone and knocked out his brains."

Her stunned husband went back to ascertain the truth, and while he was gone, she set his wagon, which was loaded with all of their store bought goods, on fire, The cover was completely burned, as were some valuable articles. When the man saw the flames, he came running back to put them out. According to Elizabeth, when this was accomplished, "The husband finally mustered spunk enough to give his wife what she needed: a good flogging."

Unfortunately, Mrs. Geer doesn't tell us what effect the whipping had on the woman, but one has to wonder if it did any good. After all, anyone who would set fire to her own wagon probably would not be deterred by a few blows from her husband.

Slavery in California

California's first Constitution was written one hundred and fifty years ago, and in it slavery was outlawed in no uncertain terms. It becomes difficult, then, to understand the events that occurred on February 7, 1850, right in the Plaza of San Jose.

The trouble in San Jose began when a white man commenced beating a black man with a stick over the head. The marshal quickly took the white man into custody and along with the black man, headed for the nearest Acalde.

When asked by the pioneer jurist to explain his actions, the white man gave the court a rationale that shocks modern sensibilities.

"That fellow is my slave," said the defendant. I brought him from home with me. When I made up my mind to leave town this evening, he refused to go, so I broke a stick over his head, which I had a right to do. He is my property, and I intend to keep him and give him a good two hundred lashes in the bargain."

The man went on to argue that, although the new Constitution excluded slavery, it did not apply to those who came here before its adoption, and the court agreed with him!

The Acalde considered the case for a moment and then in a decision that was lamented by most everyone in town, he ordered the slave to be put in jail to await his "master's orders" and in the mean time to be flogged publicly for his disobedience.

So the next day, he was taken out to the plaza where he had been beaten over the head with a stick. They stripped him to the waist, tied him up and flogged him. Then they returned him to jail.

The editor of the Alta California expressed outrage at the whole affair and got a writ of Habeas Corpus, freeing the black man, but it was too late. By the time it was served, his master had already called for him, and that ended the matter as far as the state was concerned. It didn't, however, end things for the slave. He was still considered chattel property, notwithstanding the freedom clause of the California Constitution.

Judge David S. Terry

Law and order was always difficult to maintain in the olden days - especially in San Francisco. That's why its citizens formed vigilance committees, to take the law into their own hands, and that's why Supreme Court Justice David S. Terry came to San Francisco, to put an end to mob rule. As things turned out, however, he should have stayed at home.

The San Francisco vigilance committees were established ostensibly for "the maintenance of peace and good order of society." In actuality they were nothing more than highly organized groups of mid-19th century minute men - only the enemy was not the British. It was the elected leadership of the town.

In 1856, the Vigilantes served notice on the Sheriff and his deputies that accused prisoners would be held "strictly accountable" for their crimes. The threat came through loud and clear, so the Sheriff appealed to the state. That's when Judge Terry appeared on the scene.

Now Terry had his own problems with law and order. He was generally known to be ready to fight at the drop of a hat. That's what had folks so puzzled when the Judge came to San Francisco to see that the law would prevail in the administration of justice.

It all might have worked out all right if only Terry had not been challenged by a vigilante. The hot-tempered jurist, the law and order man, settled the argument by pulling a knife and slashing his opponent. He was promptly indicted by the vigilance committee for this violent act.

Fortunately Terry's opponent did not die, and he was acquitted of any wrong doing by an official jury. The vigilantes in the meantime gave the judge a wide berth. No one was anxious to take on a proponent of law and order who would just as soon shoot you as look at you.

Judge David S. Terry went back to Sacramento and ironically in 1859 killed United States Senator David Broderick in a duel. For this Supreme Court Justice, insuring domestic tranquillity through law and order meant making the other fellow toe the mark.

San Francisco is known throughout the United States for its tolerance of diversity. Just about any cockamamie idea or movement can find a safe haven for incubation in that City. Take for instance the case of Joshua Abraham Norton. When he declared himself "Norton the First, Emperor of the United States and Protector of Mexico," San Francisco residents nodded their assent and paid homage to His Majesty for twenty-one years.

Norton came to San Francisco in 1849, already a rich man, and his wealth continued to grow until 1859,

Joshua Abraham Norton

when he lost everything in some wild rice speculation. At that point, something inside the man snapped, and he presented himself to the public as the Emperor of the United States.

Dressed in a rumpled old military uniform, Norton strode proudly into the offices of a San Francisco newspaper and gave them the notice of his self-coronation. For some reason, the editor printed it and overnight created Norton I, Emperor of the United States.

For the next two decades, Norton graced the streets of San Francisco with his presence. Citizens who passed him addressed him as "Your Majesty." Policemen saluted him smartly. He reviewed the state militia, and a special chair was always reserved for him in the state legislature. Likewise, the newspapers published a number of his imperial proclamations.

In one he abolished Congress and fired both Abraham Lincoln and Jefferson Davis.

To finance his royal affairs, Norton printed his own money, which, although legally worthless, was grabbed up by tourists at above face value. To supplement his finances, Norton I, taxed all of the businesses in town and collected the two or three dollar assessments personally.

On the night of January 8, 1880, Norton I suddenly passed away. Newspapers ran the headline, "The King is Dead." Later ten thousand people filed past his casket, and his funeral cortege was two miles long. He was buried in the Masonic cemetery and on his tombstone they engraved these words, without the quotation marks, "Norton I, Emperor of the United States and Protector of Mexico, Joshua A. Norton, 1819-1880."

It seemed a fitting monument to the man who had the gumption to proclaim himself Emperor of the United States and managed to convince an entire town to humor him for more than twenty years.

Nearly every wagon train west had the onerous duty at least once of disposing of the remains of a departed fellow traveler. For overland argonauts, it was rather simple. A hole was dug, the body was committed to the ground, and then the train moved on.

At sea, however, it was quite different, as John Letts discovered on December 6, 1849. The deceased was G.W. Ray, whose intention it had been to return to Maine from California. Needless to say, he didn't make it. He died at ten in the morning and immediately a gang-plank was made ready. It was hung over the side of the ship, supported by the rail, and a piece of canvas was thrown over it, upon which the body of G.W. Ray was placed. Someone tied a rope around the dead man's waist and then ran it down and around his ankles. To that end of the rope was tied a heavy sand bag. Then Mr. Ray was sewn up in the piece of canvas upon which he was resting. Everything was now ready.

The other passengers gathered round and the Captain read a prayer. With the final "amen," the end of the gangplank was ordered raised and down slid the corpse.

In the words of John Letts, "We were under a full press of canvas with an eight-knot breeze as the body passed gently to its watery grave. The last bubble rose to the surface, and the wind passed mournfully through the shrouds, as if sighing his last requiem."

John M. Letts was certainly no stranger to death. He had seen it first hand coming to California. But that first burial at sea was a bit unnerving, even for a California 49'er. Watching Ray's body, tethered to a sand bag, slide down a gang plank and into the sea, was enough to give rise to second thoughts about ocean travel.

Of all of the stories of overland travel during the gold rush, none is more poignant than that of J. Goldsborough Bruff and the time that he had to bury four members of his party. Before he had covered the grave, he was definitely sorry that he ever took the job.

Bruff's company had just reached the Sierra Nevada mountains on October 30, 1849, when they decided to camp for the night. Ormond Alford, his two sons, and their buddy, John Cameron pitched their tent at the base of a huge oak. About one o'clock, a storm blew the tree down, right on top of Alford's tent, killing two of the occupants instantly and mortally wounding the other two.

Captain Bruff was called upon to dig the grave, which he accomplished in short order. He wrapped the corpses in canvas and placed them in the hole. Then he made a marker out of the tail board of a wagon and scratched the following inscription:

"Ormond Alford, 54; and his sons, William, 19, and Lorenzo, 15, and John W. Cameron, aged 22. Killed by the falling of an oak tree upon them, while asleep in their tent, near this spot about 1 A.M. October 31st, 1849."

Just as Bruff was about to fill in the grave, the widow and mother wanted one more look at the deceased, so he jumped down in the hole. "I had a disagreeable task getting down in the grave," wrote Bruff, "treading between their necks, as best I could, and standing in the middle, supporting myself with one hand on the breast of the corpse, while I loosened the sheet and exposed the faces. I then scrambled out and we filled it in."

With his task finished, Bruff then added this appendix to his homemade tombstone: "Their journey is ended, their toils are all past; together they slept, in this false world, their last. They here sleep together, in one grave entombed, Just as they slept on the night they were doomed."

Harry Love

Every school child knows that Harry Love is supposed to have killed the outlaw, Joaquin Murrieta, and put his head in a jar. In the summer of 1853, newspapers all over were writing about how the California Rangers under Love had slain Murrieta. It was an ignominious end for the man whom some were calling a folk hero, but not nearly so revolting as the death of the one who received the reward for killing him.

After he collected his share of the bounty for killing Joaquin Murrieta, Harry Love settled down near Santa Cruz, California, where he married a huge, strong-willed divorcee by the name of Mary Bennett. She was tough-minded and stubborn, and after the two began to quarrel, Harry took to the bottle.

Between Mary's overbearing ways and Harry's drinking, the marriage went on the rocks. She moved to Santa Clara where she owned some property and hired a handyman by the name of Chris Everson. In a short time Chris was doing a little more than just help around the place.

On June 28, 1868, Love decided to settle the score. He rode to Mary's residence with a pistol and a shotgun and waited for her and Everson by the gate. When the couple pulled up in a buggy, Harry opened fire, and Chris did the same. A settling of the dust revealed that Everson had received some birdshot in the face and arm but was in no serious danger. Love, on the other hand, had been hit in the right arm.

A physician was called, and he decided to amputate Love's arm right there on the porch. When Harry protested, the doctor gave him a huge dose of chloroform and began to cut. Within moments the arm was off, but Harry went into shock and died.

Thus the man who allegedly cut off the head of Joaquin Murrieta was himself dismembered, and his body lies unmarked in the cemetery of Santa Clara Mission. Attempts in 1979 to erect an historical marker over his grave were abandoned because of wide-spread protests over the project. So Harry Love continues to lie unheralded in his final resting place, presumably minus an arm. Such is the verdict of history on the killer of Joaquin Murrieta whose body also lies in an unmarked grave, minus his head.

Joaquin Murrieta

Newspaperman Horace Greeley was always taken with the frontier, and he showed it with his now famous admonishment, "Go West, young man, Go West." In 1859, that's exactly what he did, but by the time he reached his destination, he wished that he had stayed at home.

Horace Greeley decided to come to California by stage coach. After crossing the plains and deserts, he reached the Sierra Nevada, and that's where he encountered the incomparable Hank Monk.

Greeley was put aboard Monk's stagecoach, and the driver was ordered to deliver him in Placerville for a 7:00 P.M. speaking engagement. Off dashed the stage with such furious speed and fearful bouncing that Greeley leaned out the window and yelled, "Sir, I don't care if we get there at seven!"

"I got my orders," intoned the driver as he whipped his horses around the spine-tingling curves. In a few minutes Greeley stuck his head out the window again and said, "I don't care if we don't get there at all."

"I got my orders," shouted Hank, driving madly on. At that moment a jarring bump sent Greeley's head crashing through the roof of the coach. "Keep your seat, Mr. Greeley," ordered the unruffled Hank Monk.

Just outside Placerville, a welcoming committee had gathered and planned on stopping the stage to take Greeley and carry him in honor to the city, but Hank had other ideas. He whipped up the team and scattered the crowd with the cry. "I've got my orders!"

So Hank Monk proudly delivered his passenger to Placerville with time, to spare, but it was a rather indecorous arrival for the refined easterner as the stage coach screeched to a stop on Main Street with Greeley's head sticking through the top. The newsman had learned very quickly that no one stood on ceremony when traveling in Hank Monk's stage. It was enough just to get there.

Horace Greeley

Theodore Judah

The prospects of building a railroad across the continent from the East Coast to California brought the Big Four into being. These high powered entrepreneurs of the Central Pacific Railroad turned a dream into a monopoly, but in the process they discarded the man who came up with the idea.

In 1853, Theodore Judah, an engineer, came to California to supervise the construction of the first railroad on the Pacific Coast. Immediately, Judah saw the possibilities of a transcontinental railroad.

One night in 1860, he held a meeting above a local hardware store in San Francisco and invited Leland Stanford, a wholesale grocer, Charles Crocker, a dry goods dealer, and Mark Hopkins and Collis P. Huntington, partners in the hardware establishment.

Before the meeting was over, the four men had committed themselves to a partnership. Stanford became the president, Huntington, vice-president, and Hopkins, treasurer. The Central Pacific Railroad Company had been formed.

Armed with this financial support, Judah convinced Congress to pass the Pacific Railroad Act of 1862, which provided for generous governmental subsidies for private railroad construction.

The Big Four, as Judah's partners were later called, wanted to build the railroad quickly, regardless of quality, so that they could begin reaping the profits. Judah resisted, so the Big Four offered to buy him out. Theodore snubbed his nose at the greedy foursome and decided to go east once again in search of capital.

Alas, as fate would have it, during the trip across Panama, Judah contracted jungle fever and died. The problem of the recalcitrant engineer had been solved without so much as a turn of the hand by the Big Four.

So the man who dreamed up the idea of a transcontinental railroad wound up on the short end of the stick, just like thousands of other pioneers in California. Small wonder that in the 19th century, folks thought the Big Four were invincible.

Linking the rails

The nation's attention was riveted on a desolate spot just north of Ogden, Utah on May 10, 1869. For the first time both sides of the continent were being linked. The completion of the first transcontinental railroad was a grand day in American history, in spite of a con-man and his victims.

After the Civil War, two giant railroads, the Central Pacific and the Union Pacific, began a race across the country towards each other, laying track. As the months slipped by, the two competitors drew closer and closer.

Finally by May 1869, it became apparent that the two companies were going to meet in Utah, so a huge celebration was prepared. Executives from both railroads were present, and it fell to Leland Stanford to drive the final ceremonial golden spike with a silver hammer.

With the crowds pressing and the officials beaming, Stanford grabbed the hammer, while a mysterious person, posing as a San Francisco jeweler, was making his way among the throng.

He passed among the onlookers taking orders for souvenir watch chains which he proposed to make from the golden spikes that were being hammered by Stanford. At five dollars each, the con-man was doing a land office business. Then it was announced that the golden spikes were going to be removed right after the ceremony, so the "jeweler" beat a hasty retreat.

Those who had succumbed to the fanciful oratory of the impostor were livid, and this helps to explain the destruction that occurred after the ceremony. Within hours of the completion of the first transcontinental railroad, those who had been bilked out of their money began to seek compensation, and they got it.

After the two golden spikes were removed by the authorities for safe keeping, under the cover of darkness, the angry victims made off with 12 regular spikes, 6 ties, and 2 pair of rails! In their rage, they had disconnected the railroad link almost as soon as it was completed.

The damage was of course repaired, and neither the con-man nor his victims were ever caught, all of which serves to remind us that very little is sacred when the masses run amuck.

Chinese immigrants in California

It was a common belief in California during the 19th century that Chinese immigrants were all addicted to opium. To be sure some of the Chinese did seem to indulge themselves in the habit, but the blame can hardly be placed at their feet. Chinese opium came to America because of the British and their taste for tea.

Actually, the British coveted a number of China's exports, such as its silk, porcelain, and spices, but it was its tea that was particularly sought.

The Chinese, on the other hand, cared for nothing British except their silver, and this of course presented England with a serious balance of trade problem. What could they find to sell the Chinese that would ease the hard currency drain on their treasury?

The answer was opium, a cash crop that flourished in British India. With the aid of some corrupt Chinese officials, a flourishing trade was soon established. British merchant ships traded chests of opium for chests of tea and silk. A number of England's largest family fortunes were soon established in this way, while the Chinese were introduced to opium.

Then came the California gold rush, and the British chickens came home to roost in the hen houses of their American cousins. Chinatowns soon popped up at all the larger diggings, and opium smoking flourished. Just as the Chinese authorities had been powerless to stop the flow of the drug into their country, Americans could only observe its effect in California.

A few grains of opium smoked in a pipe gave the beginner a feeling of euphoria. One pipe per day for ten days was enough for addiction. Once the smoker graduated to three pipes a day, any attempt at withdrawal caused chills, arm and leg cramps, diarrhea and agonizing psychic misery. A moderate smoker able to limit himself to one pipe per day could expect to live another 20 years after his first pipeful.

The heavy smoker of up to eight pipes per day would be dead within six years. Most smokers died by the age of 50, having spent two thirds of their income for opium. These sojourners in a new land definitely paid a high price so that the British could enjoy their cup of tea.

George Custer at Little Big Horn

It was the discovery of gold in the Black Hills that set the stage for the last stand of George Armstrong Custer. Thousands of miners invaded the land that had been occupied by Native Americans since time immemorial, and a severe culture clash ensued.

By the summer of 1876, an army of troops under the command of General Alfred H. Terry had been sent to answer the threats from several tribes who had concentrated in the region of the Big Horn River. Terry dispatched Custer to block the Indians' escape route into the Big Horn Mountains.

The vain and rash Custer took 250 men with him, and the history books tell us that they all perished. A closer look, however, reveals that some of Custer's men didn't die. Forty of them survived simply because the Colonel made them mad.

The foolhardy Custer set out for the Little Big Horn accompanied by thirty Arikaras, six Crow, and four Sioux Indians whom he had hired as scouts. After a quick reconnoiter, they informed Custer that he was hopelessly outnumbered and strongly urged that he wait for reinforcements.

Custer, however, always the headline seeker, did not want to share his presumed glory with anyone else and insisted on pressing forward with the attack. At that point, one of the Crow scouts shed his uniform saying that since he was going to meet the Great Spirit, he wanted to be dressed as an Indian, not a white man. An enraged Custer fired all of his Indian scouts and ordered the 210 remaining troopers forward.

When he reached the Little Big Horn, Custer ran into 2,500 Sioux led by Sitting Bull, Crazy Horse, and Rain-in-the-Face. He and his men fought bravely, but every one of them died on the spot.

We don't know what happened to Custer's Indian scouts, but one thing is for sure. They didn't die with him, although they apparently were willing to do so. In the end, their lives were saved by Custer's temper tantrum. Born of an over-zealous and reckless nature, the Colonel's cocksure attitude removed his Native American scouts from the battle. Had he been turned differently, there might have been forty more bodies to bury as a result of Custer's Last Stand.

Fate is fickle, no doubt about it. Take the case of old Chief Sitting Bull. He was the magnet that drew all of those hundreds of Indian warriors to meet Custer and his Seventh Cavalry at the Little Big Horn. Immediately after the massacre, he fled to Canada, then he returned to the United States to perform the unthinkable.

The United States was just about to celebrate its 100th birthday when it was shaken from its dogmatic slumbers. Facing an Indian army of over 2,000 warriors, led by Sitting Bull, General George Armstrong Custer and 210 of his cavalry troopers were killed in battle on June 25, 1876.

After the battle, Chief Sitting Bull and his band retreated into Canada, but the government there offered them no succor, so Sitting Bull led his tribe back across the border into the United States. On July 19, 1881, the famous chief surrendered at Fort Buford. It began to look as if his days of freedom were over, then a fellow named Buffalo Bill made him an offer he couldn't refuse.

William F. Cody, for all of his showmanship, was a true western folk hero. He was a scout, a pony express rider, and most significantly an Indian fighter. That's what makes his dealings with Sitting Bull so interesting.

In 1883, Cody conceived of the idea of organizing his famous Wild West Show, and the centerpiece of the attraction was none other than Sitting Bull. The old Chief came out of retirement to perform before crowds in the East. Thousands poured into the arenas to catch a glimpse of the man who beat Custer. Like a sideshow freak, the noble Indian leader was paraded before the audiences to the cheers and jeers of a fickle, white crowd.

The proud Chief remained stoic to the end, but in joining Buffalo Bill's Wild West Show, he revealed to the whole world how pragmatic he really was. Surely, ten years earlier, at the Battle of the Little Big Horn, he never thought that he would be re-enacting that bloodshed before delighted crowds of palefaces. The passage of years can certainly do strange things.

Chief Sitting Bull

Thomas W. Custer, Boston Custer, Lt. James Calhoun

Some remember the Battle of the Little Big Horn as Custer's Last Stand. It was on that day that the flamboyant Lt. Colonel George Armstrong Custer made a mistake that cost him dearly, and not only him but his entire family.

In late 1875, with the continued intrusions of Whites into their sacred lands in the Black Hills, hundreds of Sioux and Cheyenne Indians left their reservations with the great warrior Sitting Bull, to fight for their territory.

To force the Indians back on the reservations, the army dispatched three units. One of these included Custer and his Seventh Cavalry, which by June 1876, had managed to come upon a huge number of warriors on the Little Bighorn River.

In what was a disastrous error of judgment, Custer split his own force in three parts. One column under Captain Frederick Benteen was sent to block an escape route through the upper valley of the river. Another column under Major Marcus Reno was sent to pursue a group of Indians across the river, while Custer led the remaining 210 troopers to attack the village. Suddenly they found themselves cut off from the rest of his force and completely encircled by Indian warriors.

Every man fighting with Custer died that day. The army had to notify the families of the 210 soldiers who lost their lives, and Custer's was particularly hard hit, for not only did the brash, headline seeking officer die, two of his brothers and his brother-in-law went down with him.

Riding with George Armstrong Custer on that day were his brothers Thomas W. Custer, recipient of two Congressional Medals of Honor during the Civil War and commander of Company C of the 7th Cavalry and 28 year old Boston Custer who was a guide and teamster for the regiment. Also riding with the Custers was their brother-in-law, Lt. James Calhoun who had married their sister Margaret Custer.

After the battle was over and retribution taken on the remains of the soldiers, they were buried where they fell. Later George Armstrong Custer, Thomas Custer, Boston Custer and Lt. Calhoun were disinterred and reburied in other cemeteries back east.

It seems that they shared as much in death as they did in life. One could even make the case that, for the Custer's, fighting Indians was a family affair.

Chief Sitting Bull was a hero to his own people for a while, but in time he became a pawn to others. Even in death he couldn't preserve his dignity, for folks would just not allow his dust to settle peacefully.

After defeating Custer in the Battle of the Little Big Horn, Sitting Bull went to Canada for awhile and then returned to the United States to work for Buffalo Bill Cody in his Wild West Show.

The proud Chief remained stoic to the end, and when he died, they buried him in a rather obscure grave outside Fort Yakes, North Dakota. That's where he remained until one night in 1957, when a group of admirers from Mobridge, South Dakota crossed over in the middle of the night with a back hoe and stole his bones to give him a monument that befit their hero.

After years of ridicule and degradation, it finally appeared that Sitting Bull would be treated with respect. But then the folks in Fort Yakes lobbed a bombshell. They claimed Sitting Bull had never been moved after all! He remained right where he had been buried, at Fort Yakes. The Mobridge people, it seems, hadn't recovered the remains of the great warrior chief at all. What they got were the bones of his horse.

Chief Sitting Bull Monument

Sharkey

    Today the name of Wyatt Earp is synonymous with the Old West - you know, highwaymen, shoot-outs, and gunfights on Main Street. But it was only after Earp's death that those stories of his exploits in Wichita, Dodge City, and Tombstone, Arizona, came to the fore. While he was alive, his real claim to fame was a piece of mischief he committed at a boxing match.

San Francisco, California, was the site of the Sharkey-Fitzsimmons fight on December 2, 1896, and it just so happened that Wyatt Earp was on hand for the event. After betting heavily on Sharkey, the underdog, Earp climbed into the ring, for somebody had made him the referee.

Early in the first round, Fitzsimmons threw a punch that knocked his opponent to the floor. It looked like it was all over, and Wyatt Earp had lost a bundle of cash. That's when he played his hand. He called Fitzsimmons' punch a foul and awarded the fight to Sharkey!

The furor that rippled through town was every bit as volatile as Earp's Tombstone days. Wyatt faced a bitter public, so bitter that somebody charged the ex-marshal with fixing the fight, and he was hauled into court. The case, however, was dismissed for lack of evidence.

Then a few days later, Wyatt and Sharkey added fuel to the fires of criticism when they strolled into a local saloon together. Ironically, Fitzsimmons was there holding forth at the bar. He was informing the crowd that Wyatt Earp had robbed him of his title, and that if he ever got within punching distance, he would show Earp that a closed fist could move faster than a man could draw a gun.

Sharkey and Wyatt entered the bar just in time to hear the fighter's threats. The room got very quiet and Fitzsimmons suddenly became aware of the man standing shoulder to shoulder with him. He stumbled back a few steps as if he had been struck himself, and hastily retreated from the saloon.

From that point on, Earp's reputation grew but not necessarily as a gunfighter. Until his death in 1929, he was remembered as much for his skill at fixing a fight as he was for settling one.

Wild Bill Hickok

Wild Bill Hickok! The very mention of the name creates the image of an old west gunfighter. For more than a decade, he made his reputation by dispatching his enemies with his twin colts. Wild Bill defeated every foe. One by one his adversaries fell before him, and Hickok showed no remorse - until he faced Phil Coe. After he killed Coe, Hickok, weeping unabashedly, vowed never to fight again.

Now, there was never any love lost between Hickok and Coe. For a long time they vied with each other for the affections of Jessie Hazel, the proprietor of a high class bawdy house. In the end, however, Coe won out and decided to celebrate.

Coe and some of his friends went on a shooting spree up the main street of Abilene, Kansas, and Hickok, as marshal, was obliged to stop them. When he was challenged by Wild Bill, Coe made the mistake of drawing his gun. Both men fired twice from about eight feet. Coe missed with both shots, but Hickock put two bullets into the Texan's stomach, and he died two days later.

There can be little doubt that the marshal took some pleasure in shooting Coe, but it proved to be a tragedy in disguise. Just as Hickok was firing at Coe, another man, holding a revolver, rushed toward them. Thinking the intruder was a cohort of Coe's, Wild Bill fired twice more and killed the man. Unfortunately, the victim turned out to be Mike Williams, Hickok's deputy and close friend.

Marshal James Butler Hickok, the stone-cold killer, carried Williams into the Alamo Saloon and laid him on a billiard table. He vowed never to fight again.

Wild Bill was as good as his word, and maybe that's what made him such an easy mark for a neer-do-well like Jack McCall. In the old days he would have been ready, but on August 2, 1876, he wasn't. McCall, anxious to make a reputation for himself, shot Hickok in the back of the head from three feet while he was playing cards in a Deadwood saloon.

It has been said that those who live by the sword, die by the sword, and that appears to be true of Wild Bill Hickok. One has to wonder, however, how it would have all turned out if the gunslinger had not lost a part of himself that night, when he took the life of his very best friend.

Brigham Young

By 1850, two years after the discovery of gold in Coloma, Northern California had been transformed into a fast-growing, dynamic region. It stood in stark contrast to Southern California, which was characterized by mud huts and a hot, waterless, dusty, near desert climate. Then the Mormons showed up, and all of that changed.

Brigham Young had always wanted a settlement in the vicinity of southern California to support his state of Deseret, so that newly converted Saints arriving from Europe would have some place to gather before beginning the long trek to Salt Lake City. In 1850 he received word that two of his missionaries had found a good spot. The Isaac William's ranch was for sale. They wrote: "Here there is the soil, climate, and water to raise crops of any kind. It is situated within 40 miles of the port of San Pedro and 112 miles of San Diego."

Young appointed two Elders to head an expedition to look the ranch over. He asked for 20 volunteers to go along and got five hundred. Secretly, however, he suspected that many had been lured by the prospect of finding gold.

"I was sick at the sight of so many of the Saints running to California after the gods of this world," said Young, "and I was unable to address them."

So off they went. Their little expedition moved southward toward a little spring called Las Vegas. From there they moved through the Mojave Desert, traveling over a barren and destitute stretch and over a seven thousand-foot mountain range.

When they got to the Williams ranch, the leading elders rejected it, but continued to look around the area. They finally found the place they wanted. The Saints went to work building a split-log fort.

There was no government in the area, but the Mormons didn't worry about that. They had brought their own. A ward and a stake were set up, with its bishop and a president, and a high council to serve as a tribunal, and that's how San Bernadino, California was born. Once again the Mormons had opened up and settled a new land.

Twists

from the

Twentieth Century

Homer Plessy

Any reflection on the civil rights struggle in America quite naturally focuses on Rosa Parks. Her courage in the bus boycott in Birmingham has become a symbol of the entire movement. Ms. Parks, however, wasn't the only African-American to refuse to give up a seat on a public conveyance. Homer Plessy did the same thing, but with quite a different outcome.

Homer Plessy lived in New Orleans, Louisiana, during the latter part of the 19th century. He never dreamed that when he got into that ruckus on the street car that his action would set into motion a national policy of legal segregation, nor that the United States Supreme Court would be a party to the injustice.

It was in 1896, that Homer couldn't find a spot in the "colored" section of the New Orleans street car, so he moved on up to the "white" car. It didn't take long for the conductor to stop and have Plessy arrested for violating a state law which prohibited the mixing of the races in public accommodations.

Apparently Homer was not one to give up easily, for he challenged the constitutionality of the state statute. Nevertheless, the lower and appellate courts upheld the law, so Homer continued to push - all the way to the United States Supreme Court, where he was sure he would find a sympathetic ear.

On May 6, 1896, Homer received a stunning rebuke. In an almost unanimous decision, the Court ruled that the law requiring restaurants, hotels, hospitals, and other public accommodations to have separate facilities for Blacks was constitutional. Thus the so-called "separate but equal" doctrine of southern segregationists became the law of the land.

For the next half century, Jim Crow laws, separating Blacks from Whites in every sort of public accommodation proliferated, and every time an objection was raised, someone always pointed to the precedent set in the Plessy case. The Supreme Court had let him down. His vindication would have to come in the person of Rosa Parks who had the same courage as Homer Plessy but lived in a different time.

Rosa Parks

Titanic Survivors

It was on April 15, 1912, that the Titanic sank. Over 1200 people lost their lives, but among those who lived was Renee Harris. She was snatched from the icy waters and put safely aboard the Carpathia, her rescue ship, but even then she still had one more ironic hurdle to jump.

The days prior to the sinking had passed all too quickly for Renee. The steamer was making its way at a powerful 24 knots into the iceberg studded waters of the North Atlantic. Finally the unthinkable occurred. The ship hit a mountain of ice, and in about four hours the unsinkable liner was at the bottom of the ocean.

Renee made it to a lifeboat and for hours they rowed. Finally a shout went up. It was a ship, the Carpathia! Renee Harris' ordeal was over - almost.

The survivors were taken aboard and given every possible consideration. There were, however, limits to the hospitality that even the Carpathia could offer. Once she was aboard the rescue ship, Renee went to the wireless room to send a message to her family. Thinking now that all had been accomplished and turning to leave, Renee heard the operator say, "That will be three dollars please." Shocked, Renee tried to explain that all of her money went down with the Titanic, to which the duty-bound operator replied, "I'm sorry, Madam, but it is impossible to send ANY free messages."

Dumbstruck, Mrs. Harris stumbled back on deck. Then a Mr. Hoyt came to her rescue and gave her the money; Renee returned to the radio room, paid the three dollar fee, and her message was finally sent.

Thus it was that the Carpathia could receive a distress signal from the Titanic - speed through the icy waters at its own peril to rescue the survivors - lodge the poor unfortunates in private quarters - feed and clothe them - provide medical care - and still refuse to send a free wireless message.

Apparently there were limits to the goodwill that could be offered by the Carpathia, especially when it came to company policy on sending wireless messages. After all, business was business.

Alvin C. York

Sergeant Alvin C. York was a national hero, but not just because of his unparalleled exploits on the battlefields of World War I. He also won his place in the hearts of his countrymen for his moral stature. No one ever doubted that Alvin was a man of God. He had made a solemn promise to his mother that he would never drink, smoke or chew. He promised her that he would always live an upright life, and he held to it.

It was because of this strict moral code that he had to wrestle with his conscience when the United States entered World War I. Before he could shoulder his rifle, he had to decide whether or not he could kill another human being. This dilemma kept him up day and night, until finally he decided on the side of patriotism and marched off to battle.

Had the war been fought just a couple of years earlier, however, York would have been spared those pangs of conscience. His mother could attest to that.

After reaching the third grade, Alvin had quit school to help his father eke out a meager existence on their rugged, little family farm. For a while he followed his mother's Puritan guidance, but then he left home to work for the railroad. That was his undoing.

Alvin York learned to drink moonshine right along with the best of them. On weekends, he rarely drew a sober breath. Month after month, he would gamble his wages away. By his own admission, he stayed out late most every night and had his share of powerful fist fights without ever being whipped.

Then M.H. Russell came riding into those Tennessee mountains preaching the Gospel. Somehow Alvin York wound up at one of his meetings and was converted. Overnight Alvin York became a changed man. He became a devout Christian.

So Sergeant Alvin C. York, having disavowed his profligate life and armed with a deep and abiding faith in the Almighty, set out slaying the enemy in record numbers during World War I.

One has to wonder how things might have turned out if he had remained a drunk.

Edith Bolling Wilson

The fight for women's rights seemed to have reached its zenith when the 19th Amendment gave women the right to vote. While feminists all over the country congratulated themselves, there was one woman who was just too busy to join in the revelry. She was already functioning as President of the United States.

The President had been warned not to take the trip. His health was borderline, and he had been pushing himself. Sure enough, as his train neared Kansas, he was seized with a paralyzing stroke, and immediately his entourage headed back to Washington D. C.

While his closest advisors wrung their hands and pondered what to do, the President's wife took charge. No one was allowed to see the Chief Executive without her approval. The President's son in-law couldn't break through the protective wall erected by the strong-willed woman. Even the Vice President of the United States was ignored by this guardian of the bed chamber.

As for official business, it was up to the President's wife to determine which pieces of legislation were laid before him. Upheld by the warm, firm hand of a woman - the woman who was for all intents and purposes the President - the palsied hand of Woodrow Wilson clung to power. Edith Bolling Wilson had no personal ambitions, but she was determined that as long as her husband was breathing, he would remain the President in word and deed.

With that shaky hand, Wilson signed the few letters and documents placed before him by his wife. Everything likely to disturb his peace of mind was withheld. Even the private secretary refrained from entering the bedchamber except when sent for. He placed his memoranda on vital questions before Mrs. Wilson, leaving it to her do decide when and if they would reach the President. In effect Edith Wilson was the reigning monarch.

So it was in 1920, the year of the 19th Amendment, that Edith Bolling Wilson became, so to speak, not only the secretary to the President and acting Secretary of State. but acting President as well. Susan B. Anthony would have been proud.

Minnie Marx

Minnie was known as the woman who taught her children to be fools, and that's probably the truth, but there's much more to the story than that. While she trained her sons in the art of slapstick comedy, she also embedded in them the eternal principle of all performers, "The show must go on," no matter what.

Without the guiding hand of Minnie Marx, the world would probably have been deprived of the wonderful, zany, humor of the Marx brothers. She was their agent, their manager, their severest critic, and their most appreciative audience. She was also the force that drove them on.

It was Minnie who cajoled a neighbor to teach Chico Marx to play the piano. It was Minnie who got Groucho his first job in Gus Edwards' vaudeville act, and it was Minnie who screamed and argued for all of her sons until they finally found their niche in the entertainment world.

She lived to see an achievement greater even than her wildest hopes - the popularizing of the Marx Brothers. She went to see their first motion picture 51 times! Then came that fateful evening when her boys were playing "Animal Crackers" in New York. Mama and Papa Marx had had an early dinner and were preparing to go to the theater. Suddenly Minnie seized her husband's arm. "Give me the mirror, Sam," she said. "I think I got a stroke." She never spoke again.

A doctor was called, and the boys were advised by telephone of what had happened. Harpo, Groucho, Chico, and Zeppo didn't even have to think. They immediately set about doing the only thing their mother would have allowed them to do.

They went through the ultimate ordeal of actors - to laugh, to jest, to carry on the show - while their mother lay dying. When the final curtain had been rung down, the four clowns, still in make-up, hurried to reach their mother before it was too late.

Their father met them at the foot of the stairs and took them to her room. They stared at the lifeless form on the bed and wept over the body of Minnie Marx. They had not been in time to tell her good-bye, but they had preserved a family tradition. Never disappoint the audience. Keep the people laughing. Minnie would have been very, very proud of her boys.

Marx Family

Much has been written about baseball's infamous Black Sox Scandal. In 1919, the Chicago White Sox threw the World Series; they lost on purpose that year to the Cincinnati Reds. The eight Chicago players who cooperated with professional gamblers paid a high price for their treacherous pay-off scheme and rightly so. However, in a major miscarriage of justice, the one man who was really responsible for the scandal didn't even suffer a slap on the wrist.

Contrary to popular opinion, the gamblers didn't come to the players; the players came to them. It all started when first baseman Charles Gandil approached a well known gambler by the name of "Sport" Sullivan. A deal was struck in which Gandil would guarantee that the White Sox would take a dive in the 1919 series for $80,000.

Once the agreement was made, Gandil proceeded to line up seven more players who, with minds working in tandem, would insure that their team lost. For their cooperation, each of the players would receive $10,000.

It doesn't come as much of a surprise that Gandil instigated the scandal. The tall, muscular, rough and tough type ball player had been an ex-fighter, an ex-boilermaker and was known to be in with a number of underworld characters, mostly gamblers. What is surprising at first blush is what motivated the other seven to take a dive? The answer is plain and simple: Charles Comiskey, owner of the White Sox.

Comiskey was such a tight-fisted tyrant that he made Gandil's recruiting job a cinch. The Chicago players had really had it with Comiskey, whom they viewed as a stingy despot who demanded more and more for less and less.

Most of the other major league teams gave their players a $4 per day meal allowance; Comiskey gave $3. Often the White Sox had to play in dirty uniforms because Comiskey refused to have them cleaned.

In 1918, Comiskey forced all of his ball players to take a cut in salary because "attendance was low." The next year, however, when the White Sox were breaking attendance records, Comiskey refused to share his good fortune with the players who caused it.

Top salary on the White Sox was $6,000, while most of the players made between four and five. When a delegation approached Comiskey just before the World Series with the facts of the 1919 season, they were told to "take it or leave it." They had to take it, and that made Gandil's job relatively simple.

Although each of the players received $10,000 in ill-gotten gain, they paid a heavy price for the illegal windfall, the most devastating of which was being barred from baseball for life. Names like Shoeless Joe Jackson, Lefty Williams, and Happy Felsch became synonymous with dishonesty and double dealing.

In the meantime Charles Comiskey went right on making huge profits on the backs of his players. No one ever suggested that he shoulder his share of the blame for the scandal. In fact they even named the baseball park after him.

Sometimes History can be awfully fickle when it chooses its villains.

Benny Kubelsky

In the beginning Benjamin Kubelsky didn't appear to be destined for anything special. Nobody in his hometown saw much promise in him, especially, his father, Mayer. In fact, the Waukegan, Illinois, haberdasher became so disenchanted with his son that he fired him when the lad fell asleep while minding the store and let a phony customer steal eleven pairs of pants. When Benjamin left his father's place that day, he walked onto the stage of history, but it took a little while to get there.

Benjamin didn't have any more success in school than he had tending his father's store. It was as if all of his teachers were conspiring against him. They accused him of being more interested in the theater than in learning, and they weren't far from the mark. That is why they asked him to leave in his second year of high school.

Benjamin had been taking violin lessons since he was six, and this was his one true love. If only he could earn a living with his violin. Therefore, at the age of sixteen he applied for a chair in the Waukegan Theater orchestra. He honestly thought his rendition of "Home Sweet Home," was a knockout, but the management thought differently. At first, the most they could offer him was a job as doorman, and when he finally did make it to the orchestra pit, the theater folded up. Benjamin could do nothing but return home, hat in hand.

By his seventeenth birthday, nearly every door on which Benjamin knocked was slammed in his face, and his next venture did not appear to hold any more promise. When he announced that he was going to take his fiddle to vaudeville audiences, his father's blood boiled, and he ordered Benjamin out of his house. "All actors," he insisted, "were bums," and to make matters worse, "all actresses were immoral."

Benjamin Kubelsky was undeterred. He formed a partnership with a piano player and toured the small time for four years. Then the United States entered World War I, and his life changed forever.

Kubelsky joined the Navy and landed in the entertainment department. His job was to play his violin for the recruits at the Great Lakes Navel Station. He did his best, which was pretty good, but his performance didn't do much for the troops. They were looking for something else, and they got it when one of the officers said to Benjamin, "For God's sake, talk." Kubelsky put his fiddle under his arm and began to make fun of the Navy. He was an instant success.

As much as he loved the violin, it stayed under his arm. Benjamin Kubelsky had discovered a powerful, hidden talent. He could make people laugh. All he needed was to make a few minor changes. If he was going to appeal to a wide audience, they had to be able to pronounce his name, so he shortened it, and that's how Benjamin Kubelsky became Jack Benny.

Thus did the youngster from Waukegan finally make good. For years thereafter, from radio and television, he kept America laughing. Benjamin Kubelsky never did lose his ability as a violinist, but Jack Benny never let it show.

President Calvin Coolidge

On August sixth, 1923, Warren G. Harding died suddenly at the age of 57, and with his passing, Vice-President Calvin Coolidge ascended to the Presidency. The nation's new chief executive was something of an enigma, but he wanted it that way. Folks didn't call him "Silent Cal" for nothing.

It didn't take long for the taciturn Coolidge to win a place in the hearts of the American people with his wry wit and calm manner. In fact the nation developed something of a love affair with his pithy one-liners.

His most famous, of course, was his dictum that the "business of America is business," but second to that was an exchange he had one evening at a White House function. The President had invited the press corps to a social event, and one rather pushy reporter attempted to set Coolidge up for an interrogation. She informed Silent Cal that before coming to Washington, she had made a bet. She told the President that she had wagered she could engage him in a conversation which would consist of more than his usual yes and no responses. In fact, she told Coolidge that she had bet she could engage him in at least a three word conversation. The President eyed his young guest, leaned over, and gently replied, "You lose."

Then there was that time when someone woke him up from his customary afternoon nap. The blurry eyed President sat up, looked around and asked, "What's wrong? Isn't the country still here?"

Now the reasons given for Coolidge's terse eloquence are many, but it's best summed up by the man himself. On December 6, 1923, just prior to making the very first Presidential radio broadcast to the nation, and aware that he possessed a rather sober personality, he said, and we quote, "The American people seem to want a solemn ass as a President, and I think I'll go along with them." And that's just what Calvin Coolidge did.

With all the political hot air that's being passed around now, it's enough to make one yearn for those good old days when terseness was almost a virtue.

The Monkey Trial of 1925

When Charles Darwin began thinking about the origin of species, he raised a ruckus that continues to this very day. At no time, however, has the debate caused more controversy than in the so-called Monkey Trial of 1925. The jury in that case returned a guilty verdict, giving a leading prosecutor a thumping victory, but he never lived to enjoy it.

It all started when a high school biology teacher by the name of John Scopes decided to test a Tennessee law which prohibited public school instructors from teaching any theory that man is descended from a lower order of animal.

Scopes was immediately indicted, and brought to trial. Overnight, the entire country focused on the town of Dayton, Tennessee. The famous defense attorney, Clarence Darrow ran to help Scopes, while William Jennings Bryan, three time Presidential candidate rushed in to advise the prosecution.

The outcome of the trial was a forgone conclusion. The judge, John Raulston, was a rural magistrate from the hamlet of Fiery Gizzard, Tennessee, who was strongly prejudiced against the defendant. Scopes was found guilty of being in violation of the Tennessee law and fined $100.

The guilt or innocence of the teacher, however, was not what held the nation spellbound. The attraction of the trial lay in the gargantuan struggle between the liberal Darrow and the fundamentalist Bryan, who agreed to testify as an expert witness on the Bible.

The verdict of history is that the aging politician was no match for his cynical opponent. Through no efforts of his own, his side won the case, but there was a price. Bryan was publicly raked over the coals by Darrow and discredited in the minds of many. Not even the guilty verdict could raise his slumping spirits. After the trial, Bryan trudged home, and within a few days he died in his sleep, never having gained his self-confidence.

So the Scopes trial was the last battle for the aging warrior, but he did have the last word. He may not have convinced the skeptics, but the statute that set the stage for the "Monkey Trial" spectacle, although later ignored and unenforced, remained on the books. For a long time the state of Tennessee officially agreed with Bryan and denounced the theory of evolution, while at the same time turning a blind eye to his fundamentalist arguments.

Coach John Heisman   Heisman Tropy

Every member of the Georgia Tech football team was poised to decimate their opponents on that crisp October afternoon in 1916. Their coach had instructed them to show no mercy, and the players followed his instructions with relish. When the whistle finally blew, ending the game, the score stood at 222 to 0. Normally a coach who would allow such a massacre would become a pariah to the game. In this case, however, he became a national hero.

The high scoring game was played between Georgia Tech and Cumberland College. No one really expected Cumberland to win, but neither did they expect such a rout. From the very first, Georgia's running backs scored at will. By half time, Georgia had scored 19 touchdowns and led by 126 points.

Both teams went to their respective locker rooms to plan their strategies for the 2nd half. The record is silent about what transpired in the Cumberland shower room, but the Georgia coach's admonition to his players is well known.

Leading 126 to 0, he said, "Men, we might be in front,

but you never know what those Cumberland players have up their sleeves." He went on to urge them to continue fighting as if they were behind in the game. "Show them no mercy," he intoned. The Georgia players stormed back on the field and ran up another 96 points in the second half.

It had been a bruising embarrassment for the Cumberland players and one that should have sent the Georgia coach home, hanging his head in shame. The Georgia running backs rolled up 528 rushing yards, 220 on kickoff returns, and another 220 on punt returns. Not a single pass was thrown by Georgia.

One would have thought that the Georgia coach would have been vilified, but the contrary proved to be the case. In spite of the unconscionable drubbing his team gave Cumberland, he went on become a football hero, and as such, he left such an impact on the game that his name has become a household word.

The fact that football games are divided into four quarters can be traced directly to the Georgia Tech coach. He invented the center snap to the quarterback and came up with the "T" and "I" formations. Then in 1935, his name was immortalized.

Football officials decided that an annual trophy should be given to the most outstanding collegiate player in the country. In time it became the most prestigious award in football. They named it the Heisman Trophy after Coach John Heisman, that same Georgia Tech coach who once shut the gates of mercy on little Cumberland College. Apparently in this case, "might did make right."

Amelia Earhart

In July 1937, a gallant and skillful pilot vanished over Howland Island in the Pacific. Her name was Amelia Earhart, perhaps the best known aviatrix in the history of flight. If her public thought that she was the epitome of determination, they ought to have seen her private side. The woman had ice-water running through her veins.

Earhart had only been flying for two years when she set an altitude record for women by soaring to 14,000 feet, and she did it in a little open-cockpit plane powered by a three-cylinder air-cooled engine. Later she became the first woman passenger to cross the Atlantic by plane, and in 1932 she made history by being the first woman to actually fly solo across the Atlantic. The year before, she shocked the world by getting married. Would this be the end to America's dare devil darling? Would some man tame her? Not a chance. The same iron will that she exhibited in public also reigned in her private life.

Amelia's intended was George Palmer Putnam, and while they were waiting in his mother's home for the justice of the peace to arrive, the bride handed the groom a letter. In it, Amelia let George know just what she expected out of their marriage.

At the outset, Amelia, although she did love George, expressed some reluctance to marry. She was afraid that it would interfere with her own ambitions. "In our life together," she wrote, "I shall not hold you to any medieval code of faithfulness to me, nor shall I consider myself bound to you similarly. Please let us not interfere with each other's work or play. In this connection," she continued, "I may have to keep some place where I can go to be myself now and then, for I cannot guarantee to endure at all times the confinements of even an attractive cage." In closing, Amelia exacted what she called a cruel promise. "You must let me go in a year if we find no happiness together."

Nobody knows how Amelia's marriage to George Putnam really worked privately, but one suspects that she charted her own course in the air and on the ground. She always had and she always would. In public or in private, Amelia Earhart apparently loved her independence more than life itself.

Earl Long

Political life in Louisiana has always been a bit bizarre. For the better part of the 19th and 20th centuries, the "good old boy" system flourished, giving rise to governmental shenanigans that made the rest of the country blanch. That's why few were surprised in 1959, when they yanked the Governor right out of the capitol building and took him straight to a state mental hospital.

As fate would have it, however, he wasn't destined to remain there for long. It would take more than a few barred windows to hold this patient.

Earl Long was serving his third term as Governor of Louisiana, when in 1959 he addressed a hostile, joint session of the State Legislature. Long had been in a heated tug-o-war with the lawmakers over his attempt to succeed himself, and on this particular day, he lost his temper at the rostrum.

Most folks who owned a television set that morning watched with amazement as three men held Governor Long down in a wheelchair while they dragged him screaming, kicking, and cursing into a waiting limousine for a ride to Southeastern Louisiana Hospital in Mandeville.

When the state police arrived at the hospital, they were met by the hospital director, Dr. Charles Belcher. Knowing that he had a tiger by the tail, Belcher sought direction from the State Director of Hospitals, Jesse Bankston. The latter ordered Belcher to place the Governor under heavy lock and key.

Earl Long may have been crazy all right, but he had

access to a telephone, which meant that he could still instruct his staff, and that is exactly what he did, right after he telephoned Dr. Belcher and Bankston.

First, Long ordered Belcher to release him, and Belcher refused.

Next, the Governor directed Bankston to release him. Bankston also refused.

Then, by phone, Long directed his staff to find out if he had the authority to fire Bankston and Belcher. When the answer came back in the affirmative, those two men were suddenly unemployed.

With the opposition out of the way, the Governor then had his staff cast about for replacements who were sympathetic to his predicament. Within a few days, Long's aides found a new State Director of Hospitals and a new Director of the Southeastern Louisiana Hospital at Mandeville.

Governor Earl Long made the new appointments and in a matter of hours he was released, to no one's surprise.

A police escort was sent to the hospital to bring the Governor to a celebration breakfast with his staff at the Green Springs Motel in Covington, Louisiana. Now he was surrounded by his friends, who all along had believed in his sanity. At this point, however, Long gave his own supporters cause for pause.

When the waitress served the meal, the Governor refused to eat his own food. Instead, he took his breakfast from everyone else's plate. He was afraid someone in the group might try to poison him.

For those shocked and stunned staffers who had stood by the Governor, it was a long, lonely, and silent ride from there to the state capital, and they, along with everyone else, gave Governor Earl K. Long a wide berth until his term of office was over.

Adolf Hitler

Nearly every school child has seen those famous photographs of the Hindenburg, the most majestic of all of the German airships, reduced to flames in 1937. In the aftermath of the disaster, a multiplicity of causes were given, but few put the blame where it should have been placed - squarely on the shoulders of Adolf Hitler.

It was 7:25 on the morning of May 6, 1937, and the Hindenburg was attempting a landing at Lakehurst, New Jersey, after making its 20th transoceanic flight. As it dropped its mooring lines to the ground crew 200 feet below, the giant craft burst into flames. Twenty-seven passengers jumped to their deaths rather than face the terrifying fire.

After the official body count, 36 people were found to have lost their lives in the destruction of the Hindenburg, including one American member of the ground crew.

Following this unprecedented disaster, most of the experts blamed an atmospheric electrical spark that supposedly ignited the gas that was flowing from a leak in the ship. The fact that the outer cover of the tail section was fluttering just seconds before the explosion gave support to this theory. Still others pointed to the high volatility paint used on the airship, which would have been something akin to coating it in rocket fuel.

All of these scientific explanations, however, fail to take note of the political climate of the time, and herein we may find the ultimate cause of the burning of the Hindenburg.

The huge blimp had been designed to be lifted by helium. This gas, however, was scarce at the time, and the United States refused to sell any to Germany, which had just been taken over by the extremist, Adolf Hitler. The American Government suspected that the Germans might soon have military plans for their airships. Thus, the Hindenburg was forced to turn to the highly flammable gas, Hydrogen, seven million cubic feet of it, instead of helium. One has to wonder if the Nazi dictator, whose bellicose rantings and ravings spread fear throughout the world, wasn't at least indirectly responsible for the destruction of his own airship.

Herman Talmadge

In 1946, the people of Georgia went to the polls to elect their governor. It was a forgone conclusion that the Democratic nominee would win, since the Republicans didn't even field a candidate. That is why the supporters of Eugene Talmadge prepared for the election with confidence. Little did they know that when the post-election dust settled, Georgia would have three governors instead of one.

The name of Talmadge had been synonymous with power politics in the state of Georgia for a long, long, time. They were unbeatable in state wide elections, then came 1946.

In that year Georgia amended its Constitution and allowed for the people to elect a Lieutenant Governor. Eugene Talmadge easily won the top spot for the fourth time, but the people chose Melvin Thompson, an anti-Talmadge man to be their first Lieutenant Governor.

Everyone knew at the time that Talmadge wasn't in the best of health, so when he died before the January 1947

Inauguration Day, his supporters went to plan B. They convinced the state legislature to pass a bill allowing that body to elect the governor in case the office fell vacant. It came as no surprise that they chose Eugene Talmadge's son, Herman Talmadge, to take his father's place.

At that juncture, Melvin Thompson, the duly elected Lieutenant Governor cried foul. He stepped forth to claim the Governor's office. If Eugene Talmadge had died after he had been sworn in, there would have been no question; Thompson would have taken his place. Since, however, Talmadge died before the inauguration, legal ambiguity created a political vacuum, which was filled by the legislature.

The situation then took a strange turn. The outgoing Governor, Ellis Arnall, announced that until the situation was cleared up, he would not relinquish his office. Now Georgia had three governors.

While Governor Thompson turned to the courts for support, Governor Herman Talmadge and Governor Ellis Arnall conducted a comic opera in the capitol building.

Governor Talmadge ordered state troopers to eject Governor Arnall from his office. When the latter had been safely escorted home, Talmadge seized control of the Governor's office. Meanwhile, Arnall returned and opened up his own Governor's office in exile in a kiosk in the capitol.

For the next two months, Georgia's three governors began to appoint government officials, and chaos reigned. Finally in March 1947, the Georgia Supreme Court stepped in and ruled that Melvin Thompson was the rightful governor, but he didn't last long. The courts also ordered a special election, and Herman Talmadge won that one hands down.

From that point, things continued as they had for years. The Talmadge machine had beaten back another assault on their political hegemony. The enduring aspect of the entire farce, however, was that the people of Georgia were treated to a sideshow that they never forgot.

Adolf Hitler

In the late 1930s, Americans stood at the crossroads. In Europe, a paper-hanging corporal was mesmerizing Germany. Goosestepping storm troopers marched the streets with arms outstretched in an act of obeisance. Sabers rattled, and America prepared. If only fate had played its trump card when it had the chance, Adolf Hitler might have been laughed off the stage of history instead of terrorizing the world.

The Nazi dictator was the grandson of a wandering miller, Johann Hitler, who plied his trade from village to village in Lower Austria. The elder Hitler lived a rather Bohemian existence, especially when it came to his relations with women, and in late 1836, he took up with a peasant woman from the village of Strones named Maria Anna. On June 7 of the next year, without benefit of clergy, Maria gave birth to a son, whom she named Alois.

Upon assessing his situation, Johann beat a hasty retreat. Alois, meantime, was baptized with his mother's name and raised by his father's brother.

Then, after an absence of 39 years, Johann Hitler reappeared. His brother had died, leaving a small estate, to which Alois would have some claim if he could prove that he was a Hitler.

At the prospect of sharing in his son's inheritance, Johann finally did the right thing. In the presence of three witnesses and a notary, he testified that he was indeed the father of Alois. The parish priest scratched out Alois's last name on the baptismal record and inserted the name Hitler.

From that day forward, Alois never used his mother's name again. Now he was legitimized as Alois Hitler, and when his son Adolf was born, instead of Schicklgruber, He was christened Adolf Hitler.

Had it not been for the tardy action of his grandfather, Adolf Hitler would have been born Adolf Schicklgruber, and that raises an interesting question. Could the Nazi leader have galvanized the masses with the last name of Schicklgruber? There are those who think not.

"Heil Hitler" became the obligatory form of greeting between Germans during the Third Reich. How would the masses have reacted to a demand for "Heil Schicklgruber?" Perhaps if old Johann Hitler had remained out of sight, the sound of Adolf Schicklgruber would have produced nothing but giggles among the German people.

Henry Ford (L) with son, Edsel

1938 was a banner year for Adolf Hitler. The Nazi leader marched his soldiers into Austria and Czechoslovakia, without so much as a tip of the hat to the Western Democracies, and awarded the Grand Cross of the German Eagle to two of his supporters.

The first German Cross went to Benito Mussolini for the role he played in convincing France and England not to oppose Hitler's move to take over his two smaller neighbors. The second went to an American industrialist who had been a supporter of Fascism in Germany for a long time.

According to Germany's representative to the U.S., the American had given Adolf Hitler financial backing when he was first starting out in politics. Later, Winifred Wagner, daughter of composer Richard Wagner, made pleas for funds for the National Socialist movement in Germany and convinced the famous American to come up with the cash.

The American continued to support Hitler as he consolidated his hold on Germany and built up his military forces. Then in that fateful year of 1938, he was awarded and accepted the German Cross. Ostensibly, he was recognized by the German Fuhrer for "making motor cars available for the masses," but in reality Hitler gave him the Cross for opening an assembly plant in Berlin for the purpose of supplying trucks to the German Army.

The Grand Cross for the Order of the German Eagle was Nazi Germany's highest honorary award given to foreigners. To receive his, Mussolini had to travel to Berlin, but the American had his, complete with a personal congratulatory message from Adolf Hitler, bestowed on him at home by the German Ambassador.

Thus it was that Henry Ford, one of America's pioneer industrialist - the first to apply assembly line manufacturing to the mass production of affordable automobiles - the man who gave us the Model A and the Model T shared the spotlight on the eve of World War II with Benito Mussolini, as Adolf Hitler acknowledged his debt to American ingenuity.

Viewed in this context, we can begin to understand why Ford proclaimed that "History is bunk!" The man didn't know where he was going because he didn't know where he had been.

General Theodore Roosevelt Jr.

On June 6, 1944, Allied troops hit the beaches of Normandy to begin a drive across France and into Germany. While some American troops left their landing crafts at Omaha Beach and fought their way across the sand to put a stop to the withering German machine gun fire, those soldiers who had been assigned to Utah Beach encountered a different kind of problem. Due to a navigational error, they landed on the wrong inlet on Utah Beach. Thankfully they had a battle hardened Brigadier General to lead them in correcting the mistake.

Instead of allowing panic to set in, the troops followed their leader without hesitation, for they knew that he was the first Allied General to wade ashore on the entire Normandy beachhead. It had taken two verbal requests and one written message from the fighting General to Headquarters before he had been allowed to accompany his troops in the Utah

Beach landing. Once they became organized after missing their assigned landing point, the General became a veritable lightning rod of leadership. What soldier wouldn't follow such a man?

Quickly assessing the situation and seizing the initiative and advantage, the fighting General directed the remainder of the division into the "new sector" by yelling, "We'll start the war from here!" He and his troops overwhelmed the German defenses and rapidly drove inland. They then proceeded to outflank the Germans on their initial objective, clear the entire beachhead, and link up with the airborne assault forces with fewer casualties than any of the divisions on the other four beachheads. Armed only with a pistol and walking with a cane due to arthritis, the General led several assaults along the beachhead in what then Lieutenant General Omar N. Bradley, commander of the US 1st Army and of the overall amphibious operation, would later describe as the single bravest act he witnessed in the entire war.

Bradley wasn't the only one who noticed the bravery of the fighting General that day. So highly esteemed were his exploits on the beach, that five weeks later word came that he had been promoted to Major General and reassigned to command another division. Unfortunately, he would never be able to assume his new assignment, for on the day the message came, the fighting General died of a heart attack.

They buried him on the battlefield of Normandy, and back in the States his widow accepted his Medal of Honor from her husband's distant cousin, President Franklin Delano Roosevelt, who said simply, "His father would have been proudest," and indeed he would have been. General Theodore Roosevelt Jr. had more than matched his father's charge up San Juan Hill by choosing to lead his men himself through the horrors of the invasion of Normandy.

Aldrich, Lorenzo D. <u>A Journal of the Overland Route to California & the Gold Mines</u>. Los Angeles: Dawson's Book Shop, 1950.

Apostol, Jane. <u>El Alisal, Where History Lingers</u>. Los Angeles: Historical Society of Southern California.

Audubon, John Woodhouse. <u>Audubon's Western Journal, 1849-1850</u>. Tucson, Arizona: The University of Arizona Press, 1984.

Bailey, Thomas A. <u>The American Pageant</u>. Volume I. Boston: D.C. Heath and Company, 1966.

Bailey, Thomas A. <u>The American Pageant</u>. Volume II. Boston: D.C. Heath and Company, 1966.

Bates, Ed Bryant. <u>True Tales of Outlaws & Rogues</u>. Coarsegold, California: .45 Caliber Publishing, 2001.

Berenger, Clara. "The Woman Who Taught Her Children to Be Fools." <u>America: An Illustrated Diary of its Most Exciting Years</u>. Valencia, California: American Family Enterprises, Inc., 1973.

Bernard, Bruce. <u>Century</u>. London: Phaidon Press Limited. 1999.

Bieber, Ralph P. (ed.) The Southwest Historical Series, Vol. VII: <u>Exploring Southwestern Trails 1846-1854</u>. Glendale, California: The Arthur H. Clark Company, 1938.

Bieber, Ralph P. (ed.) The Southwest Historical Series, Vol. XII: <u>Analytical Index</u>. Glendale, California: The

Arthur H. Clark Company, 1943.

Bieber, Ralph P. Southern Trails to California in 1949. Philadelphia: Porcupine Press, 1974.

Billington, Ray Allen. The Far Western Frontier. New York: Harper & Row Publishers, 1956.

Billington, Ray Allen. The Protestant Crusade: 1800-1860. Gloucester, Massachusetts: Holt, Rinehart, & Winston, Inc., 1963.

Billington, Ray Allen. Westward Expansion. New York: The Macmillan Company, 1967.

Botkin, B.A. (ed.). Civil War Treasury of Tales, Legends, & Folklore. New York: Promontory Press, 1960.

Bruff, J. Goldsborough. Gold Rush. Vol II. New York: Columbia University Press, 1944.

Bryant, Edwin. What I Saw in California. Santa Ana, California: The Fine Arts Press, 1936.

Capps, Benjamin. The Great Chiefs. Alexandria, Virginia: Time-Life Books, 1975.

Carruth, Gorton. Encyclopedia of American Facts & Dates. New York: Harper & Row, 1987.

Catton, Bruce. The American Heritage New History of the Civil War. New York: Penguin Books, 1996.

Caughey, John Walton. Gold is the Cornerstone. Berkeley, California: University of California Press, 1948.

Chan, Sucheng. This Bitter-Sweet Soil. Los Angeles: University of California Press, 1986.

Chinn, Thomas W. (ed.) A History of the Chinese in California. San Francisco: Chinese Historical Society of America, 1969.

Clark, Thomas D. Frontier America. New York: Charles Scribner's Sons, 1959.

Cole, Martin and Welcome, Henry (eds.). Don Pio Pico's Historical Narrative. Glendale, California, The Arthur H. Clark Company, 1973.

Constable, George. (ed.). The Trailblazers. Alexandria, Virginia: Time-Life Books, 1973.

Current, Richard N., Freidel Frank, and Williams, T. Harry. American History: A Survey. New York: Alfred A. Knopf, 1967.

Daniels, Jonathan, Daniels. The Devil's Backbone. New York: McGraw-Hill Book Company, 1962.

DeVoto, Bernard. The Year of Decision, 1846. Boston: Little, Brown and Company, 1943.

Dillon, Richard H. The Gila Trail: The Texas Argonauts and the California Gold Rush. Norman, Oklahoma: University of Oklahoma Press, 1984.

Dillon, Richard. Captain John Sutter: Sacramento Valley's Sainted Sinner. Santa Cruz, California: Western Tanager Press, 1967.

Donald, David and Randell, J.G. The Civil War and
       Reconstruction. Boston: D.C. Heath and Company,
       1961.

Dowdey, Clifford and Manarin, Louis H. (eds.). The
       Wartime Papers of R.E. Lee. Boston: Little, Brown,
       and Company, 1961.

Drury, Clifford M. Marcus and Narcissa Whitman and the
       Opening of Old Oregon. Glendale, California: The
       Arthur H. Clark Company, 1973.

Drury, Clifford M. Marcus Whitman, M.D. Caldwell, Idaho:
       The Caxton Printers, Ltd., 1937.

Egan, Ferol. The El Dorado Trail. New York: McGraw-Hill
       Book Company, 1970.

Etter, Patricia. To California on the Southern Route, 1849.
       Spokane, Washington: The Arthur H. Clark Company,
       1998.

Evans, George W.B. Mexican Gold Trail. San Marino,
       California: The Huntington Library, 1945.

Ferguson, Rebecca N. The Handy History Answer Book.
       Detroit: The Visible Ink Press, 2000.

Foote, Shelby. The Civil War: Fort Sumter to Perryville. New
       York: Random House, 1958.

Forbis, William H. The Cowboys. Alexandria, Virginia:
       Time-Life Books, 1973.

Freehling, William W. The Road to Disunion. New York:

Oxford University Press, 1990.

Garraty, John A. The American Nation. New York: Harper & Row, 1966.

Garrison, Webb. Brady's Civil War. Guilford, Connecticut: The Lyons Press, 2000.

Gillenkirk, Jeff, and Motlow, James. Bitter Melon: Inside America's Last Rural Chinese Town. Berkeley, California: Heydey Books, 1987.

Grant, Ulysses S. Grant. The Civil War Memoirs of Ulysses S. Grant. New York: A Tom Doherty Associates Book, 2002.

Greeley, Horace. An Overland Journey. New York: Alfred A. Knopf, 1964.

Grun, Bernard. The Timetables of History. New York: Simon & Schuster, 1982.

Hafen, Leroy R., Hollon, W. Eugene, and Rister, Carl, Coke. Western America. Englewood Cliffs, New Jersey: Prentice-Hall, Inc., 1970.

Hagerty, Donald J. Desert Dreams: The Art and Life of Maynard Dixon. Layton, Utah: Gibbs-Smith Publisher, 1993.

Hague, Harlan and Langum, David J. Thomas O. Larkin. Norman, Oklahoma, University of Oklahoma Press, 1990.

Handlin, Oscar. America: A History. New York: Holt,

Rinehart and Winston, 1968.

Hardeman, Nicholas Perkins. Wilderness Calling. Knoxville, Tennessee: The University of Tennessee Press, 1977.

Harwell, Richard B. (ed.). The Civil War Reader. New York: Mallard Press, 1957.

Hittell, Theodore. History of California. San Francisco: Pacific Press Publishing House, 1885.

Holbrook, Stewart, H. The Old Post Road. New York: McGraw-Hill Book Company, Inc., 1962.

Holiday. J.S. The World Rushed In. New York: Simon and Schuster, 1981.

Hollon, W. Eugene. Beyond the Cross Timbers. Norman, Oklahoma: University of Oklahoma Press, 1955.

Hollon, W. Eugene. The Southwest: Old and New. New York: Alfred A. Knopf, 1961.

Horsman, Reginald. The Frontier in the Formative Years, 1783-1815. New York: Holt, Rinehart and Winston, 1970.

Hunt, Thomas. Ghost Trails to California. New York: Weathervane Books, 1976.

Johnson, William Weber. The Forty-Niners. Alexandria, Virginia: Time-Life Books, 1974.

Karolevitz, Robert F. Newspapering in the Old West. Seattle, Washington: Superior Publishing Company, 1965.

Klose, Nelson. A Concise Study Guide to the American Frontier. Lincoln, Nebraska: University of Nebraska Press, 1964.

Kowalewski, Michael. (ed.). Gold Rush: A Literary Exploration. Berkeley, California: California Council for the Humanities, 1997.

Lamar, Howard R. (ed.). The Reader's Encyclopedia of the American West. New York: Thomas Y. Crowell Company, 1977.

Lapp, Rudolph M. Blacks in Gold Rush California. New Haven: Yale University Press, 1977.

Latta, Frank F. Joaquin Murrieta and his Horse Gangs. Santa Cruz, California: Bear State Books, 1980.

Levy, JoAnn. They Saw the Elephant. Hamden, Connecticut: Archon Book, 1990.

Lothrop, Gloria Ricci and Nunis, Doyce B. Jr. (eds.) A Guide to the History of California. New York: Greenwood Press, 1989.

Maino Jeannette Gould. Left Hand Turn: A Story of the Donner Party Women. Modesto, California: Dry Creek Books, 1987.

McDonald, Archie P. William Barrett Travis: A Biography. Austin, Texas: Eakin Press, 1995.

McPherson, James M. Battle Cry of Freedom. New York: Ballantine Books, 1988.

Miller Francis Trevelyan. (ed.). The Photographic History of the Civil War in Ten Volumes. New York: The Review of Reviews Co., 1911.

Mitchell, Broadus. Heritage from Hamilton. New York: Columbia University Press, 1957.

Morgan, Ted. Wilderness at Dawn. New York: Simon & Schuster, 1993.

Muir, Andrew Forest. Texas in 1837. Austin: University of Texas Press, 1958.

Myres, Sandra L. (ed.) Ho for California! San Marino, California: Huntington Library, 1980.

Nadeau, Remi. Ghost Towns & Mining Camps of California. Santa Barbara, California: Crest Publishers, 1965.

Nevin, David. The Texans. Alexandria, Virginia: Time-Life Books, 1975.

Nevins, Allan. Fremont: Pathmarker of the West. Lincoln, Nebraska: University of Nebraska Press, 1939.

Newell, Chester. History of the Revolution in Texas. New York: Arno Press, 1973.

Nunis, Doyce B. (ed) The Bidwell-Bartleson Party: 1841 California Emigrant Adventure. Santa Cruz, California: Western Tanager Press, 1991.

Paul, Rodman. Mining Frontiers of the Far West, 1848-1880. New York: Holt, Rinehart and Winston, 1963.

Pitt, Leonard. The Decline of the Californios. Berkeley: University of California Press, 1966.

Pomeroy, Earl. The Pacific Slope. New York: Alfred A. Knopf, 1966.

Rolle, Andrew F. California: A History. New York, Thomas Y. Crowell Company, 1963.

Rolle, Andrew. John Charles Fremont. Norman, Oklahoma: University of Oklahoma Press, 1991.

Schlesinger, Arthur, M. Jr. The Cycles of American History. Franklin Center, Pennsylvania: The Franklin Library, 1986.

Schlissel, Lillian. Women's Diaries of the Westward Journey. New York: Schocken Books, 1982.

Seagraves, Anne. Soiled Doves: Prostitution in the Early West. Hayden, Idaho: Wesanne Publications, 1994.

Secrest, William B. California Desperadoes. Clovis, California: Word Dancer Press, 2000.

Secrest, William B. Lawmen & Desperadoes. Spokane, Washington: The Arthur H. Clark Company, 1994.

Secrest, William B. Perilous Trails, Dangerous Men. Clovis, California: Word Dancer Press, 2002.

Shirer, William L. The Rise and Fall of the Third Reich. New York: Simon and Schuster, 1960.

Slatta, Richard W. Cowboys of the Americas. New Haven:

Yale University Press, 1990.

Smithwick, Noah. The Evolution of a State or Recollections of Old Texas Days. Austin: University of Texas Press, 1987.

Sosin, Jack M. The Revolutionary Frontier, 1763-1783. New York: Holt, Rinehart, and Winston, 1967.

Steckmesser, Kent Ladd. The Westward Movement: A Short History. New York: McGraw-Hill Book Company, 1969.

Stewart, George R. The California Trail. New York: McGraw-Hill Book Company, Inc., 1962.

Stone, Irving. Clarence Darrow for the Defense. New York: Doubleday and Company, Inc., 1941.

Stone, Irving. From Mud-Flat Cove to Gold to Statehood. Clovis, California: Quill Driver Books, 1999.

Stone, Irving. Men to Match My Mountains. New York: Doubleday & Company, 1956.

Stone, Ted. 100 Years of Cowboy Stories. Red Deer, Alberta, Canada: Red Deer College Press, 1994.

Tanner, Ogden. The Ranchers. Alexandria, Virginia: Time-Life Books, 1977.

Trachtman, Paul. The Gunfighters. Alexandria, Virginia: Time-Life Books, 1974.

Turner, Frederick Jackson. The Frontier in American History.

Franklin Center, Pennsylvania: The Franklin Library, 1977.

Turner, Frederick Jackson. The United States 1830-1850. Gloucester, Massachusetts: Peter Smith, 1958.

Wallace, Robert. The Miners. Alexandria, Virginia: Time-Life Books, 1976.

Webb, Walter, Prescott. History as High Adventure. Austin: The Pemberton Press, 1969.

Werner, M. R. "William Jennings Bryan: The Last Battle." America: An Illustrated Diary of its Most Exciting Years. Valencia, California: American Family Enterprises, Inc., 1973.

Wharton, Clarence. History of Fort Bend County. San Antonio, Texas: The Naylor Company, 1939.

Wheat, Frank. California Desert Miracle. San Diego, California: Sunbelt Publications, 1999.

Wheeler, Keith. The Railroaders. Alexandria, Virginia: Time-Life Books, 1973.

Whitsell, Leon O. One Hundred Years of Freemasonry in California. San Francisco: Griffin Brothers, Inc., 1950.

Worcester, Don. Pioneer Trails West. Caldwell, Idaho: The Caxton Printers, Ltd. 1985.

Young, Judy, Dockery and Young, Richard. Outlaw Tales. Little Rock, Arkansas: August House Inc., Publishers, 1992.

A

B

C

D

E

F

Look for these exciting additions to the
Twist in Time series:

"The Spoken Truth"

a four CD audio book adventure featuring Bill Coate
narrating his spell binding tales of mystery and intrigue.

NOVEMBER 2005

"Looking at History"

A two disk DVD set that features thirty episodes presented
by Bill Coate from his popular syndicated television show.

JANUARY 2006

VISIT YOUR LOCAL BOOKSTORE OR ORDER
ONLINE AT
www.TWISTINTIME.com

OR CALL OUR 24 HOUR ORDER LINE AT
1-888-439-7258.

VISIT US ONLINE AT

WWW.TWISTINTIME.COM

YOU WILL FIND

Chapter Excerpts
Audio Excerpts
Electronic Newsletters
Original Author Articles
Book Tour Information
Maps, Timelines and Quizzes
Plus much more

www.TWISTINTIME.com

The "Past" can repeat itself.
You don't have to wait.
Pick up the book that started it all...

"History's Mysteries Revealed"
A *"Twist in Time"* series
By Bill Coate

A flavorful introduction to Bill Coate's vignette style of
teaching us today's lessons of the past.

www.twistintime.com

HISTORY PUBLISHING GROUP, INC. PRESENTS

"History's Mysteries Revealed"
A *"Twist in Time"* series
By Bill Coate

DUE IN STORES
APRIL, 2007

turn the page for a preview of what's to come...

Lucky Toner was a man of the sea. He earned his living as a crew member on several large ocean liners. On May 7, 1915, Lucky made history when the ship on which he was working was shot out from under him. It was a harrowing experience which he most assuredly could have avoided if only he had been one of those folks who believed that disasters come in threes.

Toner was a fireman on the Lusitania in 1915. He was working below in the ocean going sweat shop when suddenly a tremendous shock shook the ship. It had been hit by a German torpedo at the bow end of the bridge and suffered a tremendous hole torn in her side. Immediately he called out to his mates. "Come on, get up to the top. This torpedo has done us in!"

Lucky made for the top side immediately, just in time to escape the second explosion which killed many of his co-workers who were still at the furnaces. Within a few minutes the vessel was on its way to the bottom of the ocean.

From the time that he arrived on deck, Lucky Toner worked untiringly in helping women and children into the life boats. As the Lusitania listed to starboard and her masts were lowered towards the water, he climbed one of them but soon got into difficulty. He became entangled in the lines, and barely cut himself free before the ship disappeared.

He was thrown into the water but was quickly pulled onto a capsized life boat. During the time he was on there, he rendered assistance to the nine other people with whom he shared the upturned boat, six of whom were women.

Toner and his companion's fnally made it to Kinsale where dry clothing and medical aid awaited them. Then they were besieged by reporters, and that's when those who had been saved with Toner found out just how amazing his story really was.

Not only had he survived the sinking of the Lusitania, he had cheated death at sea on two other occasions. He had been a fireman on the Titanic when it went down in 1912, and lived to tell about it. Two years later, he was a crew member on the Empress of Ireland when it sank in the St. Lawrence River and killed a thousand people. Now for the third time, he had thumbed his nose of Poisidon.

When interviewed by reporters, Toner was quoted as saying, "This is the third big shipping disaster I have been in, and if I am in another, I think it will be my last. After going down with the Titanic, the Empress of Ireland, and the Lusitania, one would think that Lucky Toner would consider the third time a charm and not abuse his nickname.

When Oscar Folsom, a Buffalo, New York attorney, chose young Grover Cleveland as his law partner in 1863, most folks thought that he had made a good choice. The younger barrister was hard-working, smart, and loyal to a fault. In fact, Cleveland was so loyal that after Oscar's death in a buggy accident in 1875, he embraced his partner's family as his own. He promised the Widow Folsom that he would take real good care of her and her eleven year-old daughter, Frances. In time the whole world found out that the future President was every bit as good as his word.

Grover Cleveland, who became the administrator of Folsom's estate and unofficial guardian of his daughter, took his responsibilities seriously. He saw to his adopted family's every need and grew ever closer to Folsom's widow, Emma, and her daughter, who called their family provider, "Uncle Cleve."

Over the years Cleveland began to climb the political ladder. In 1881, he was elected Mayor of Buffalo and later Governor of New York, but he never allowed his official duties to diminish his devotion to Emma and Frances. He paid for the daughter's education at private schools, academies, and eventually to Wells College, and he saw to it that Emma wanted for nothing.

Then in 1884, the unthinkable happened. A Democrat was elected President of the United States. For the first time since 1856, the people turned their backs on the Republicans, and they did so by voting for Grover Cleveland.

In March 1885, Cleveland moved into the White House, but he soon found out he required a help mate. He could handle the duties of the Presidency, but he needed a First Lady. Naturally his mind went back to Buffalo.

He had only been President for five months when he sent for Emma and Frances. The official word was that he was simply inviting old friends to visit the White House, but the press corps couldn't be fooled. They suspected that the

President would be making a proposal for marriage, and they were right. When they reported the gossip, the country went positively giddy. Emma would make a charming First Lady, and her beautiful long-haired daughter - what a glamorous addition to the White House she would make.

Grover Cleveland did offer that proposal for marriage, and when he sent Emma and Frances on a tour of Europe, the reporters followed them, eagerly trying to scoop each other as to the wedding date. Little did they know what the White House had in store for them.

When Emma and Frances returned, Cleveland made the official announcement. There was going to be a marriage in the White House. The nation was finally going to get a First Lady, but it wasn't going to be the Widow Folsom. It was going to be her daughter!

On June 2, 1886, forty-nine year-old Grover Cleveland married twenty-one year-old Frances Folsom in a White House ceremony, and in doing so, the groom set a number of precedents. He was the first President to be married in the White House. He was the first President who could honestly say he met his future bride while she was still wearing diapers, and he was the first President to actually provide his future wife with a baby stroller in which she could ride.

Grover Cleveland may not have robbed the cradle, but he sure did rock it.

Bill Coate is the author of the Twist in Time series; *Twist in Time: "History's Mysteries Revealed"*, and *Twist in Time: "History's Shocking Secrets."* He is a national award-winning historical author, educator and speaker.

Bill Coate founded the *Madera Method* – named by his mentor, renowned author, Irving Stone - a primary source research program for elementary students and the *Madera Method Wagon Train*, which takes students along the historic western wagon trails.

Bill was named *"National History Teacher of the Year"* by the Daughters of the American Revolution, received the *Disney American Teacher Award* and was a *"California Teacher of the Year"* finalist.

Bill is a resident of Madera, California. His historical vignettes are syndicated on television and radio and appear in several daily newspapers.